TITLE:

Wix Website Builder:

A Step-by-Step Guide for Wix Website Design & Logo Maker

By

Josh Hawkins

INTRODUCTION

In today's digital-first world, having a compelling online presence is no longer optional—it's essential. Your website is often the first point of contact for potential customers, clients, or followers, making it a critical part of your success. Wix offers a powerful platform that combines simplicity with flexibility, allowing anyone to build a professional website, regardless of technical expertise.

This book is designed to be your companion on the journey to mastering Wix. We'll explore the platform's core features and advanced capabilities, providing you with the tools and knowledge needed to create a stunning website that performs at its best. Whether you're starting from scratch or looking to optimize an existing site, you'll find valuable insights here to elevate your website-building skills.

Title:

Introduction

Foreword

Chapter 1: Introduction to Wix

   Overview of the Wix Platform

   Choosing the Right Plan for Your Needs

   Exploring the Wix Dashboard

Chapter 2: Getting Started with Website Design

   Selecting and Customizing Templates

1. Business and Services

2. Online Stores

3. Blogs and Forums

4. Creative Arts and Photography

5. Personal and Portfolio

   Understanding Wix Editor and Wix ADI

3. Target Audience

   Basic Web Design Principles for Beginners

Chapter 3: Website Navigation and Structure

   Creating Intuitive Menus and Submenus

   Designing a Logical Site Hierarchy

   Enhancing User Experience with Navigation Tools

Chapter 4: Customizing Visual Elements

   Choosing and Customizing Fonts for Readability

   Working with Colors and Themes

o Blue: Trust, professionalism, and calmness.

o Red: Passion, urgency, and excitement.

o Green: Growth, health, and tranquility.

2. Custom Themes

1. Buttons and CTAs

2. Backgrounds and Images

1. Contrast Ratios

2. User Feedback

    Integrating Images, Videos, and Graphics

Chapter 5: Enhancing Website Performance

    Optimizing Load Times and Website Speed

1. Large Images and Media Files

2. Unoptimized Code

3. Server Response Time

4. Too Many Plugins or Widgets

    Ensuring Mobile Compatibility and Responsiveness

    Monitoring Uptime and Website Security

Chapter 6: Building an E-Commerce Store

    Setting Up Product Pages and Categories

    Configuring Payment Gateways and Currencies

    Managing Inventory and Order Fulfillment

    Creating a Customer-Friendly Checkout Experience

Chapter 7: Advanced Website Features

    Incorporating Social Media Integrations

    Utilizing Widgets and Plugins for Extended Functionality

Creating Membership Areas and Subscription Services
Chapter 8: Search Engine Optimization (SEO) Basics
　　Understanding SEO and Its Importance
　　Optimizing Content and Meta Tags
　　Leveraging Wix SEO Tools for Better Rankings
Chapter 9: Analytics and Performance Tracking
　　Setting Up Google Analytics
　　Understanding Key Website Metrics and KPIs
o High bounce rates? Redesign landing pages.
　　Analyzing User Behavior and Traffic Sources
Chapter 10: Launching and Maintaining Your Website
　　Conducting Thorough Pre-Launch Checks
　　Publishing the Website and Announcing the Launch
　　Implementing a Content Update Strategy
　　Monitoring and Responding to User Feedback
Chapter 11: Troubleshooting and FAQs
　　Understanding Common Website Issues
　　Wix Support and Community Resources
　　Staying Updated with Wix Features
Conclusion

FOREWORD

In a world where digital engagement is paramount, Wix has emerged as a game-changer for individuals and businesses seeking to establish a professional online presence. As someone who has witnessed the transformative power of user-friendly website builders, I am thrilled to introduce **Wix website builder**, a book that demystifies web development and empowers users to create impactful websites.

Through this guide, you will discover how to leverage Wix's extensive suite of tools to bring your vision to life. Whether you aim to launch an online store, create a blog, or promote your services, this book will provide you with a roadmap to success. Prepare to embark on a rewarding journey that combines creativity, strategy, and technology.

CHAPTER 1: INTRODUCTION TO WIX

Overview of the Wix Platform

The Rise of Website Builders

In today's digital-first era, having an online presence is essential. However, not everyone has the time or technical expertise to master complex coding languages like HTML, CSS, or JavaScript. Enter Wix—a platform that revolutionizes website building by offering a user-friendly, drag-and-drop interface. Designed for individuals and businesses alike, Wix makes it possible to create professional-looking websites without writing a single line of code.

What Sets Wix Apart?

Unlike many basic website builders, Wix stands out due to its vast array of customization options, templates, and advanced features. Whether you're an entrepreneur, artist, or blogger, Wix provides the tools you need to design a site that reflects your unique vision. With over 500 customizable templates and a robust App Market, Wix empowers users to integrate essential functionalities such as online booking, e-commerce, and customer relationship management (CRM).

Key Features of the Platform

1. **Drag-and-Drop Editor:** Wix's intuitive editor allows users to rearrange elements effortlessly. You can position text, images, and widgets exactly where you want them, ensuring full creative control.

2. **Extensive Template Library:** From professional portfolios to online stores, Wix's templates cater to diverse industries and purposes.

3. **Wix Artificial Design Intelligence (ADI):** For those seeking a fast start, Wix ADI uses AI to create a tailored website based on your answers to a few simple questions.

4. **App Market:** Enhance your website with powerful apps ranging from SEO boosters to live chat tools.

5. **Mobile Optimization:** Every template is mobile-responsive, ensuring your site looks great on any device.

Who Can Benefit from Wix?

Wix is ideal for small businesses, freelancers, and individuals seeking a professional website without the cost of hiring a developer. Whether you're launching a personal blog, showcasing a portfolio, or opening an online store, Wix provides the flexibility and functionality to meet your needs.

The Importance of a Professional Online Presence

A well-designed website can elevate your brand, improve customer trust, and increase visibility in search engines. Wix simplifies this process, allowing you to focus on growing your business while the platform handles the technical aspects of website creation.

How Wix Compares to Other Platforms

While competitors like Squarespace and WordPress offer similar services, Wix distinguishes itself through its ease of use and extensive design freedom. Its drag-and-drop functionality appeals to users who want more control over their site's layout without the steep learning curve associated with other platforms.

Understanding Wix's Limitations

Although Wix is a powerful tool, it's essential to understand its boundaries. For instance, while the platform excels in design flexibility, it may not be the best choice for highly complex websites requiring extensive back-end customization. Additionally, users seeking deep e-commerce capabilities may find the platform less robust compared to specialized platforms like Shopify.

Tips for Getting Started on Wix

- **Explore the Templates:** Spend time browsing Wix's templates to find one that aligns with your brand.

- **Leverage Wix ADI:** If you're short on time, let Wix ADI handle the heavy lifting and generate a site layout for you.

- **Familiarize Yourself with the Editor:** Take advantage of Wix's tutorials and guides to master the drag-and-drop interface.

- **Utilize the App Market:** Enhance your website's functionality by integrating apps tailored to your business needs.

CHOOSING THE RIGHT PLAN FOR YOUR NEEDS

Understanding the Wix Pricing Structure

One of the first steps in your journey with Wix is choosing a plan that aligns with your specific needs. Wix offers a variety of pricing tiers, each tailored to different user types, ranging from personal bloggers to large-scale business owners. These plans are broadly categorized into two groups: **Website Plans** and **Business & eCommerce Plans**.

- **Website Plans** are ideal for users who want to create a website without eCommerce functionality. These plans typically focus on providing ample storage, ad-free browsing, and access to essential tools for personal or professional websites.

- **Business & eCommerce Plans**, on the other hand, are designed for individuals or businesses looking to sell products or services online. These plans include features like secure payment processing, advanced analytics, and the ability to accept online payments.

Key Features Across Plans

Each plan comes with a distinct set of features. Here's a breakdown of what to expect:

- **Free Plan**: Great for getting started, this plan

includes basic Wix features but displays Wix ads and lacks a custom domain.

- **Combo Plan**: Perfect for personal use, it removes Wix ads, offers a custom domain, and provides adequate storage for small sites.
- **Unlimited Plan**: Ideal for freelancers or small businesses, this plan provides increased storage and additional tools like visitor analytics.
- **Pro and VIP Plans**: These plans cater to users seeking priority support and professional branding tools.
- **Business Plans**: These tiers offer everything from payment processing to advanced eCommerce solutions, including abandoned cart recovery and subscription services.

Evaluating Your Website's Purpose

Before selecting a plan, it's crucial to evaluate your website's purpose. Ask yourself:

1. **What type of content will you feature?** If you're showcasing a portfolio or running a blog, a Website Plan may suffice.
2. **Do you plan to sell products or services?** If so, a Business & eCommerce Plan is essential.
3. **How much traffic do you anticipate?** For high-traffic websites, consider a plan that offers greater bandwidth.
4. **What level of customization do you require?** Higher-tier plans often include advanced design and functionality tools.

Analyzing Your Budget

Understanding your financial constraints is vital when choosing a plan. Wix's flexible pricing ensures there's an option for everyone, but balancing cost with the features you need is key. Remember that opting for annual billing often provides a discount compared to monthly billing, offering long-term savings.

Consideration for Future Growth

While a basic plan might be sufficient for your initial needs, it's wise to think ahead. For instance, if you anticipate scaling your business or adding eCommerce capabilities in the future, it's worth investing in a plan that accommodates growth. Wix allows seamless upgrades, but starting with a more comprehensive plan can save time and effort down the line.

Additional Costs to Keep in Mind

Beyond the standard plan pricing, consider potential additional costs such as:

- **Premium Apps**: Some advanced functionalities may require third-party apps with separate fees.

- **Domain Registration and Renewal**: While some plans include a free domain for the first year, renewal costs apply afterward.

- **Email Marketing Services**: Tools like Wix Ascend can enhance your marketing but come with an extra cost.

Making an Informed Decision

Choosing the right Wix plan is more than a financial decision; it's about aligning the platform's capabilities with your vision for your website. By understanding your immediate and long-term goals, you can select a plan that provides the tools and resources you need to succeed.

Practical Tips for Maximizing Your Chosen Plan

Once you've selected a plan, make the most of it by:

1. **Exploring All Available Features**: Take time to familiarize yourself with the tools included in your plan.
2. **Utilizing Customer Support**: Wix offers comprehensive support, including tutorials and live chat, to help you navigate any challenges.
3. **Monitoring Your Website's Performance**: Use the built-in analytics tools to track visitor behavior and refine your site accordingly.

EXPLORING THE WIX DASHBOARD

The Wix Dashboard is your central hub for managing all aspects of your website. Whether you're setting up a personal blog, a professional portfolio, or an online store, the dashboard provides a streamlined interface to access tools, monitor performance, and enhance user experience. Here's a comprehensive look at how to navigate and leverage the dashboard for maximum efficiency.

Understanding the Main Dashboard Layout

When you first log into your Wix account, you are greeted by a dashboard designed for simplicity and functionality. It is divided into key sections:

- **Site Overview**: This section offers a snapshot of your website's current status. Here, you can view site analytics, such as visitor numbers and engagement metrics, at a glance.

- **Quick Actions**: Common tasks like editing your site, viewing site history, or managing your domain are accessible from this section.

- **Notifications and Alerts**: Wix provides real-time updates on your site's performance and any tasks that need attention, such as unprocessed orders or unpublished changes.

Customizing Your Dashboard for Efficiency

Wix allows users to personalize the dashboard according to their specific needs. You can prioritize frequently used tools and hide less relevant sections. To customize:

1. **Click on the gear icon** located in the top-right corner of any dashboard section.
2. **Select 'Edit Layout'** and drag the widgets to your preferred position.
3. **Save changes** to retain your personalized setup.

This customization ensures that essential features remain front and center, streamlining your workflow.

Key Tools Available in the Dashboard

1. **Site Editor**:
   The Site Editor is the heart of your website creation process. Access it directly from the dashboard to update content, tweak design elements, or add new pages.
2. **App Market**:
   Enhance your website's functionality with the Wix App Market. From SEO boosters to live chat tools, you can install and manage apps seamlessly through the dashboard.
3. **Analytics & Reports**:
   For those interested in performance metrics, this section provides detailed insights into traffic sources, user behavior, and conversion rates. The data-driven reports help refine your strategy.
4. **Marketing Tools**:
   Whether you're launching email campaigns or

running Facebook ads, Wix's built-in marketing suite simplifies outreach efforts. The dashboard allows you to track campaign performance in real-time.

5. **Billing and Payments**:
For e-commerce sites, this tool helps manage payment settings, track revenue, and process refunds.

Navigating Between Multiple Sites

If you manage multiple websites under a single Wix account, the dashboard provides seamless navigation. Use the dropdown menu at the top of the dashboard to switch between sites quickly. Each site's dashboard is independently customized, so your workflow remains optimized for each project.

Troubleshooting Common Issues via the Dashboard

The dashboard includes a Help Center for troubleshooting common issues. Access:

- **FAQs** and step-by-step guides for resolving typical problems.
- **Live chat support** for immediate assistance.
- **Community forums** where you can seek advice from other users.

Tips for First-Time Users

1. **Explore Slowly**: Familiarize yourself with each dashboard section. The intuitive design ensures you won't feel overwhelmed, but taking time to explore will help you make the most of the tools.
2. **Use Tutorials**: Wix offers in-dashboard video

tutorials tailored to each feature. These are particularly helpful for beginners.

3. **Bookmark Important Sections**: Save time by bookmarking frequently used tools for one-click access.

CHAPTER 2: GETTING STARTED WITH WEBSITE DESIGN

Selecting and Customizing Templates

A website's design is the first impression visitors get, making it essential to choose the right template and tailor it to meet your needs. Templates serve as the foundation of your site, providing structure, style, and functionality that can be customized to reflect your brand's identity.

Understanding the Role of Templates

Templates are pre-designed layouts that define the visual structure of your website, including elements like fonts, colors, and page layouts. These templates cater to various industries and purposes, such as e-commerce, personal blogs, portfolios, and corporate sites. By starting with a template, users save significant time compared to designing a site from scratch.

Factors to Consider When Selecting a Template

Choosing the right template involves evaluating your website's goals and your target audience's expectations. Here are key factors to consider:

- **Purpose of the Website**: Identify whether the site is for personal branding, selling products, or showcasing creative work.

- **Industry-Specific Needs**: Templates often cater to specific industries, ensuring relevant features and design elements are pre-included.
- **Ease of Navigation**: Ensure the template supports intuitive navigation, providing a seamless user experience.
- **Mobile Responsiveness**: Since a significant portion of web traffic comes from mobile devices, select templates optimized for various screen sizes.

Exploring Template Categories

Website builders often categorize templates to help users find suitable options quickly. Some common categories include:

1. **Business and Services**
2. **Online Stores**
3. **Blogs and Forums**
4. **Creative Arts and Photography**
5. **Personal and Portfolio**

Each category offers templates designed with specific functionalities, like integrated galleries for photographers or product showcases for online retailers.

Customizing Templates for Unique Branding

Once a template is chosen, customization is crucial to align it with your brand's identity.

Adjusting Colors and Fonts

Consistency in color schemes and typography is essential for brand recognition. Use your brand colors across all elements, such as headers, buttons, and backgrounds.

Similarly, select fonts that convey your brand's tone, whether professional, playful, or modern.

Incorporating Logos and Visual Elements

Your logo is a visual anchor for your brand. Place it strategically on your website—typically in the header—to ensure visibility. Additionally, use high-quality images and icons that align with your site's theme.

Modifying Layouts and Sections

Templates provide default layouts for pages, but most allow you to rearrange or resize sections. For example, you can expand the homepage's hero section to highlight your value proposition or adjust product grids for better visibility.

Utilizing Built-in Design Tools

Website builders typically offer a suite of design tools to further personalize templates. Some of these tools include:

- **Drag-and-Drop Editors**: Simplify the process of placing and resizing elements.
- **Animation Features**: Add subtle animations to create a dynamic user experience.
- **SEO Settings**: Customize meta titles and descriptions to improve search engine visibility.
- **Advanced Styling Options**: Tweak CSS for greater design flexibility.

Previewing and Testing Customizations

Before finalizing your design, it's essential to preview and test the website across various devices and browsers. This ensures:

1. **Responsive Design**: Elements scale correctly on

mobile, tablet, and desktop.

2. **Functionality**: Links, buttons, and forms work as expected.

3. **Aesthetic Consistency**: Colors, fonts, and layouts maintain uniformity across pages.

Common Pitfalls to Avoid in Template Customization

Customization is an exciting process, but it's easy to make missteps. Here's what to watch out for:

1. **Overloading with Features**: Adding too many elements can clutter the site and slow down performance.

2. **Inconsistent Styling**: Ensure uniformity in font sizes, colors, and spacing to avoid a disjointed look.

3. **Ignoring Accessibility**: Use readable fonts and ensure adequate contrast to make your site inclusive for all users.

UNDERSTANDING WIX EDITOR AND WIX ADI

Creating a website involves balancing creativity and functionality. Wix offers two main tools to simplify this process: the Wix Editor and Wix ADI (Artificial Design Intelligence). Each tool caters to different user needs, making website building accessible to everyone, regardless of technical expertise.

Overview of Wix Editor

The Wix Editor is a robust platform for those who prefer complete control over their website's design and functionality. It features a drag-and-drop interface that enables users to place elements precisely where they want them.

1. **Customizable Design Elements**
   Users can modify every aspect of their website, from layouts and color schemes to fonts and animations. This level of customization allows for unique and personalized designs.

2. **User-Friendly Interface**
   The interface is intuitive, featuring a toolbar and menus that provide easy access to all essential functions. Even without prior experience, users can quickly grasp how to navigate the editor.

3. **Wide Range of Templates**
   The Wix Editor provides hundreds of templates tailored to various industries. Whether you're

creating a portfolio, a blog, or an online store, the templates serve as a starting point for customization.

4. **Advanced Features for Flexibility**
   Advanced users can leverage tools like Corvid by Wix (now known as Velo) for custom coding, offering greater flexibility for dynamic websites.

Exploring Wix ADI

For those looking for a quick and hassle-free way to get online, Wix ADI offers an innovative solution. This tool uses artificial intelligence to create a fully functional website based on user inputs.

1. **Ease of Setup**
   Wix ADI simplifies the initial setup process by asking users a series of questions about their business or personal goals. Based on the responses, it generates a tailored website.

2. **Automated Design**
   With Wix ADI, the design process is automated, allowing users to focus on content rather than layout. The tool selects suitable fonts, images, and colors, ensuring a professional look.

3. **Editable Results**
   After the ADI generates a site, users can still make adjustments to suit their preferences. This combination of automation and flexibility is ideal for beginners or those short on time.

4. **Seamless Integration of Features**
   ADI integrates essential features, such as contact forms and social media links, ensuring the website is functional right from the start.

Comparison: Wix Editor vs. Wix ADI

Understanding the differences between these tools helps users choose the best one for their needs.

1. **Customization vs. Speed**
   - **Wix Editor**: Offers more customization options but requires more time and effort.
   - **Wix ADI**: Provides a faster setup with less customization.

2. **Control vs. Automation**
   - **Wix Editor**: Ideal for those who want full control over every detail.
   - **Wix ADI**: Perfect for users who prefer a hands-off approach.

3. **Target Audience**
   - **Wix Editor**: Suited for users with a creative mindset who enjoy building from scratch.
   - **Wix ADI**: Best for individuals or businesses seeking a quick, professional online presence without much technical input.

Best Practices for Using Wix Tools

1. **Plan Your Website's Purpose**
   Define the primary goal of your website before choosing a tool. Whether it's for e-commerce, blogging, or showcasing a portfolio, your choice will affect the design process.

2. **Utilize Templates Wisely**

Even with customization, starting with a relevant template can save time and provide design inspiration.

3. **Test Before Publishing**
Both Wix Editor and ADI offer preview modes to test your website's functionality and appearance on various devices.

4. **Leverage Tutorials and Support**
Wix provides extensive resources, including tutorials, to help users maximize these tools.

BASIC WEB DESIGN PRINCIPLES FOR BEGINNERS

Creating a visually engaging and user-friendly website requires a foundational understanding of web design principles. This section delves into the essential concepts to help beginners craft effective and aesthetically pleasing websites.

The Importance of Layout and Structure

A well-organized layout is the backbone of any website. The layout not only determines how information is presented but also influences the user experience.

- **Visual Hierarchy:** Arrange content in a way that directs the user's attention to the most critical elements first. Use larger fonts for headings, bold text for emphasis, and contrasting colors to highlight call-to-action buttons.
- **Whitespace Utilization:** Incorporate ample whitespace to create a clean and uncluttered look, enhancing readability and focus.
- **Grid Systems:** Utilize grid systems to ensure alignment and consistency. Grids help balance the visual weight of different elements across the page.

Color Theory and Consistency

Colors play a crucial role in evoking emotions and reinforcing brand identity.

- **Choosing a Color Palette:** Stick to a cohesive color scheme, typically involving a primary, secondary, and accent color. Tools like Adobe Color can assist in selecting harmonious combinations.
- **Contrast and Accessibility:** Ensure sufficient contrast between text and background for readability. High-contrast designs benefit users with visual impairments, adhering to accessibility standards.
- **Brand Consistency:** Consistently use brand colors across all pages to strengthen visual identity and recognition.

Typography and Readability

The right choice of fonts and their application significantly affect how users interact with your content.

- **Selecting Web-Safe Fonts:** Choose fonts that are legible and widely supported across different devices and browsers, such as Arial, Verdana, or Google Fonts.
- **Font Size and Line Spacing:** For body text, a font size of 16px and appropriate line spacing (1.5 times the font size) ensures readability.
- **Limit Font Variations:** Stick to a maximum of two to three fonts per website to maintain a cohesive look.

Navigation and User Experience (UX)

Intuitive navigation is essential for guiding visitors through your site effortlessly.

- **Clear Menu Structure:** Use descriptive labels and organize menu items logically. A primary menu should include key sections, while a footer menu can house secondary links.
- **Breadcrumbs and Search Bars:** Incorporate breadcrumbs for easy backtracking and search bars to enhance findability.
- **Mobile-Responsive Menus:** Ensure menus are optimized for mobile devices with collapsible or hamburger-style designs.

Responsiveness and Mobile-First Design

With mobile usage surpassing desktop, a responsive design approach is non-negotiable.

- **Fluid Grids and Flexible Images:** Employ fluid grid layouts and set image dimensions in relative units (percentages) rather than fixed pixels.
- **Touch-Friendly Elements:** Buttons and links should be large enough for easy tapping, with ample spacing to avoid accidental clicks.
- **Test Across Devices:** Regularly test your site on various screen sizes and resolutions to ensure consistent performance.

Effective Use of Media

Multimedia elements such as images, videos, and

animations enrich the user experience when used thoughtfully.

- **Optimized Media Files:** Compress images and videos to reduce load times without sacrificing quality. Tools like TinyPNG or Squoosh can help.
- **Alt Text for Images:** Provide descriptive alt text for images to improve accessibility and SEO.
- **Strategic Placement:** Position media elements strategically to support content, break up text, and maintain user engagement.

Call-to-Action (CTA) Design

CTAs guide users toward desired actions, such as subscribing to a newsletter or purchasing a product.

- **Clarity and Urgency:** Use action-oriented language, e.g., "Sign Up Today" or "Get Started Now."
- **Prominent Placement:** Position CTAs above the fold or at the end of key content sections to maximize visibility.
- **Visual Distinction:** Design buttons with contrasting colors and hover effects to make them stand out.

Accessibility and Inclusivity

Building an inclusive website ensures that all users, regardless of ability, can access and navigate your content.

- **Keyboard Navigation:** Ensure all interactive elements are accessible via keyboard.

- **Screen Reader Compatibility:** Use semantic HTML tags and ARIA (Accessible Rich Internet Applications) landmarks to improve screen reader functionality.
- **Accessible Forms:** Label form fields clearly and provide error messages that specify the issue and how to resolve it.

SEO Fundamentals for Beginners

While design primarily focuses on aesthetics and usability, incorporating basic SEO principles ensures that your website reaches a broader audience.

- **Meta Tags and Descriptions:** Write concise meta descriptions that summarize page content effectively.
- **Optimized Headings:** Use heading tags (H1, H2, H3) hierarchically for better content organization and SEO ranking.
- **Alt Text and Keywords:** Integrate keywords naturally into alt text and content without overstuffing.

Testing and Iteration

A website is never truly "finished"; continuous testing and improvements are vital.

- **A/B Testing:** Experiment with different design elements (e.g., button colors or layouts) to determine what works best.
- **User Feedback:** Collect feedback via surveys or usability testing to identify pain points and

areas for enhancement.

- **Performance Monitoring:** Use tools like Google Analytics to track user behavior and make data-driven design adjustments.

CHAPTER 3: WEBSITE NAVIGATION AND STRUCTURE

Creating Intuitive Menus and Submenus

Why Website Navigation Matters

Navigation plays a critical role in user experience, guiding visitors to find the information they need efficiently. A well-structured menu not only enhances usability but also impacts search engine optimization (SEO) by making content easily accessible to search engines.

Understanding the Basics of Menu Design

Menus serve as the roadmap for your website. They help organize content into categories, ensuring that users don't feel overwhelmed. An intuitive menu reduces bounce rates and increases user engagement.

- **Primary Navigation Menus**
  These are usually located at the top of a website and contain the main categories or pages. Examples include "Home," "About Us," "Services," and "Contact."

- **Secondary Navigation Menus**
  Found in footers or sidebars, these menus often include supplementary links such as "Privacy Policy" or "Terms of Service."

Best Practices for Creating Menus

1. **Keep It Simple**
   Avoid clutter. Limit the number of menu items to 5-7, ensuring users can scan options quickly.
   Example: Instead of listing every service separately, group them under a "Services" dropdown.

2. **Use Descriptive Labels**
   Clear, action-oriented labels like "Get Started" or "Learn More" provide a better user experience than vague terms like "Miscellaneous."

3. **Prioritize Important Pages**
   Place the most visited or important pages (e.g., "Contact" or "Shop") in prominent menu positions.

Designing Submenus for Enhanced Usability

Submenus appear when a user hovers over or clicks a main menu item. They help organize subcategories without overloading the main menu.

- **Organize Hierarchically**
  Ensure logical flow by nesting related pages under their respective parent categories.
  Example: "Products" > "Electronics" > "Smartphones."

- **Avoid Too Many Levels**
  Limit the depth of submenus to two levels to prevent users from feeling lost.

Using Visual Cues for Better Navigation

Icons, separators, and hover effects can make menus more user-friendly. For example:

- **Icons:** Small visuals next to menu items can

enhance understanding.

- **Hover Effects:** Change in background color when a user hovers over a menu item can provide instant feedback.

Testing and Iterating Menu Design

Once the menu is set up, conduct user testing. This helps identify any pain points in navigation and allows for continuous improvements based on user feedback.

DESIGNING A LOGICAL SITE HIERARCHY

What is a Site Hierarchy?

A site hierarchy is the organizational structure of your website. It dictates how pages relate to each other, ensuring that visitors can easily navigate between sections and find the information they need. An effective hierarchy improves both user experience and search engine optimization (SEO).

Importance of a Logical Hierarchy

A well-thought-out hierarchy benefits your website in multiple ways:

- **Improves User Experience:** Visitors can easily navigate and find relevant information without confusion.
- **Enhances SEO Performance:** Search engines favor well-structured websites, making it easier to rank higher in search results.
- **Simplifies Future Updates:** A logical layout facilitates easier updates and scalability as your site grows.

Key Principles of Designing a Site Hierarchy

1. Start with Your Main Goals

Identify the primary purpose of your website. Whether it's to sell products, share information, or generate leads, your goals will influence your hierarchy.

- **Example:** For an e-commerce site, the main goal is likely to sell products. Your hierarchy should prioritize product categories and a seamless checkout process.

2. Group Related Content

Organize similar content into categories or sections. This grouping helps users locate related information without jumping between unrelated pages.

- **Example:** A blog site can categorize posts by topic, such as "Technology," "Health," or "Travel."

3. Limit the Number of Top-Level Categories

Too many top-level categories can overwhelm visitors. Aim for a manageable number, typically between 4-7 categories, depending on the size and complexity of your website.

4. Plan for Scalability

Design your hierarchy with growth in mind. Your structure should allow for the addition of new categories or pages without disrupting the existing layout.

Steps to Create a Logical Site Hierarchy

Step 1: Outline Your Content

Create a list of all the pages and content your website will include. Group similar items and think about how users might look for them.

Step 2: Build a Sitemap

A sitemap is a visual representation of your site's structure. It includes main categories, subcategories, and individual pages. Tools like Lucidchart or even simple paper sketches can help in planning your sitemap.

Step 3: Create Intuitive Menus

Menus are the primary way users interact with your hierarchy. Ensure they are:

- **Clear and Descriptive:** Use labels that make sense to your audience.
- **Consistent Across Pages:** Maintain uniformity to avoid confusing users.
- **Prioritized by Importance:** Place the most crucial links in prominent positions, such as the top navigation bar.

Step 4: Implement Breadcrumb Navigation

Breadcrumbs show users their location within the site hierarchy. They not only improve navigation but also boost SEO by providing clear paths for search engines.

Step 5: Test Your Hierarchy

Before launching, test your site's hierarchy with real users. Gather feedback on ease of navigation and adjust accordingly.

Best Practices for Navigation Design

1. Use Simple Labels

Avoid jargon or overly creative labels. Visitors should understand menu items at a glance.

2. Limit Depth Levels

Keep the hierarchy shallow. Ideally, users should reach their desired content within 3-4 clicks.

3. Include a Search Bar

A search bar acts as a safety net for users who may not follow your hierarchical structure. It ensures quick access to any page.

4. Optimize for Mobile Navigation

Design menus that are mobile-friendly. Use collapsible menus and ensure touch-friendly navigation.

Common Mistakes to Avoid

- **Overloading Menus:** Too many items in a menu can overwhelm users and make navigation difficult.
- **Inconsistent Terminology:** Using different terms for the same category across the site can confuse visitors.
- **Ignoring User Behavior Data:** Regularly analyze site usage data to identify areas where users may struggle and refine your hierarchy accordingly.

ENHANCING USER EXPERIENCE WITH NAVIGATION TOOLS

Effective navigation is the cornerstone of any user-friendly website. It ensures visitors can easily access the information they need, improving engagement and reducing bounce rates. Navigation tools provide the roadmap users follow, guiding them seamlessly through the site. Whether your goal is to showcase products, share content, or capture leads, a well-structured navigation system is key to achieving it.

The Importance of Logical Site Hierarchy

A logical site hierarchy lays the foundation for an intuitive navigation system. It helps organize content in a way that mirrors how users think and search for information. A typical hierarchy includes primary pages such as Home, About, and Contact, with subcategories branching off as needed.

- **Primary Navigation Bar**: This is often placed at the top of the website and includes links to the most important pages.
- **Secondary Navigation Elements**: These might include sidebars, dropdown menus, or footers that guide users to less prominent but still essential areas of the site.

Designing a User-Centric Navigation System

User-centric design focuses on creating a navigation experience tailored to the audience's needs. Here are a few principles to consider:

1. **Simplicity**: Avoid overwhelming users with too many options. A streamlined menu is easier to navigate.
2. **Consistency**: Keep the navigation structure uniform across all pages. Inconsistent menus can confuse users and lead to frustration.
3. **Predictability**: Users should be able to anticipate where a link will take them based on its label.

Navigation Tools to Enhance User Experience

1. Search Bars

A search bar is an essential tool, especially for content-heavy websites. It allows users to quickly find specific information without having to browse through multiple pages. For optimal usability, the search bar should be prominently placed and include features like auto-suggestions and filters.

2. Breadcrumb Navigation

Breadcrumbs provide a secondary navigation aid, showing users their current location on the site relative to the home page. This feature is particularly useful for websites with deep hierarchies, as it helps users backtrack easily.

3. Dropdown Menus

Dropdown menus are effective for displaying subcategories under main menu items. They save space while allowing users to explore additional content. However, they should be designed carefully to avoid being cumbersome or confusing.

4. Sticky Navigation Bars
A sticky navigation bar remains visible as users scroll down the page. This feature improves usability by keeping key navigation options accessible at all times, especially on content-rich pages.

5. Mega Menus
Mega menus are advanced dropdowns that showcase a wide range of options at once. They're ideal for e-commerce sites or platforms with diverse offerings, as they help users quickly locate specific categories or products.

Enhancing Accessibility in Navigation
Accessibility should be a priority when designing navigation tools. This ensures that your website is usable by people with disabilities, such as those who rely on screen readers.

- **Descriptive Link Text**: Instead of generic terms like "Click here," use descriptive text that conveys where the link leads.
- **Keyboard Navigation**: Ensure that all navigation elements can be accessed via keyboard shortcuts.
- **ARIA Landmarks**: Use ARIA (Accessible Rich Internet Applications) roles to define page sections, making it easier for screen readers to interpret the content.

Testing and Improving Navigation
After implementing your navigation system, it's essential to test its effectiveness. Tools like heatmaps and user

session recordings can provide insights into how visitors interact with your site. Key performance indicators (KPIs) such as bounce rate, average session duration, and page views per session can also highlight areas for improvement.

Common Navigation Pitfalls to Avoid
While enhancing navigation, it's crucial to steer clear of common mistakes that could hinder the user experience:

- **Overcrowded Menus**: Too many menu items can overwhelm users and make decision-making difficult.
- **Hidden Key Links**: Vital pages like Contact or FAQ should never be buried under multiple layers of navigation.
- **Broken Links**: Regularly check and update links to ensure they lead to the correct pages.

CHAPTER 4: CUSTOMIZING VISUAL ELEMENTS

Choosing and Customizing Fonts for Readability

Fonts are a cornerstone of effective web design. They influence how your content is perceived and directly impact the readability and overall user experience. Beyond aesthetics, the right font can ensure that your message is accessible to a diverse audience, including those with visual impairments.

Understanding Font Categories and Their Uses

Fonts fall into several categories, each serving specific purposes:

- **Serif Fonts**: Classic and formal, often used for traditional businesses or educational websites.
- **Sans-Serif Fonts**: Clean and modern, ideal for digital platforms and startups.
- **Monospace Fonts**: Technical and precise, commonly seen in code snippets or tech-oriented content.
- **Script and Decorative Fonts**: Artistic and elaborate, best for headings or special occasions, but should be used sparingly to maintain

readability.

How to Choose Fonts for Optimal Readability

1. Consider Your Audience and Brand Identity

The font choice should align with your brand's tone and target audience. For example, a tech company might prefer a minimalist sans-serif, while a wedding planner could use elegant script fonts for headings.

2. Prioritize Legibility

- Avoid overly complex or decorative fonts for body text.
- Ensure sufficient spacing between characters (kerning) and lines (leading).
- Test font sizes to guarantee readability across devices.

3. Pairing Fonts Effectively

Combining fonts can enhance visual interest and structure. Stick to two or three complementary fonts:

- Use one for headings and another for body text.
- Ensure contrast but maintain harmony in style.

Customizing Fonts Using Web Design Tools

Most website builders provide extensive font customization options. Here's a step-by-step approach to refining your fonts:

1. Accessing Font Libraries

Website platforms typically offer a variety of fonts:

- Google Fonts: Open-source and versatile.
- Platform-Specific Fonts: Exclusive options provided by the website builder.

2. Adjusting Font Settings

- **Size and Weight**: Tailor the thickness and size for emphasis.
- **Color and Contrast**: Ensure the text stands out against your background.
- **Styling and Alignment**: Italicize or bold certain elements to draw attention.

3. Implementing Responsive Typography

Modern web design requires fonts to adapt seamlessly to different screen sizes. Use tools to:

- Set minimum and maximum font sizes.
- Employ relative units (e.g., em or rem) for scalability.

Ensuring Accessibility in Typography

Accessibility is essential for an inclusive website. Consider the following:

- **Contrast Ratios**: Maintain high contrast between text and background.
- **Readable Fonts for Dyslexia**: Sans-serif fonts like Arial or Verdana are more readable for individuals with dyslexia.
- **Keyboard and Screen Reader Compatibility**: Ensure users can navigate and read text easily using assistive technologies.

Testing and Iterating Your Font Choices

1. Gather User Feedback

Conduct usability testing to see how real users interact with your fonts. Pay attention to:

- Readability across devices.
- User preferences for font style and size.

2. Analyze Performance Metrics

Track metrics like time spent on page and bounce rates. Poor readability can lead to high bounce rates.

3. A/B Testing

Experiment with different font combinations and styles. Monitor which versions perform better in terms of user engagement and readability.

Best Practices for Maintaining Consistency

Consistency in typography ensures a cohesive design. Apply a unified style guide:

- Define font hierarchy for headings, subheadings, and body text.
- Use consistent sizes and weights across similar elements.

WORKING WITH COLORS AND THEMES

Understanding the Role of Colors in Web Design
Colors play a crucial role in shaping a website's identity and user experience. They influence emotions, perceptions, and decision-making. A well-thought-out color scheme can convey professionalism, evoke trust, or create a sense of excitement, depending on your website's goals.

1. **Psychology of Colors**
   Different colors evoke different emotions and associations:
     - **Blue**: Trust, professionalism, and calmness.
     - **Red**: Passion, urgency, and excitement.
     - **Green**: Growth, health, and tranquility.

2. **Choosing a Color Scheme**
   A cohesive color scheme ensures visual harmony. Tools like color wheels or online platforms such as Adobe Color can help you choose complementary or analogous colors that enhance your website's appeal.

Applying Themes for Consistency
Themes provide a unified look and feel by combining specific colors, fonts, and design elements. They simplify customization and ensure that all pages of your website

maintain a consistent aesthetic.

1. **Pre-Designed Themes**
   - **Ease of Use**: Pre-designed themes offer ready-made solutions for different industries.
   - **Customization Options**: While themes provide a starting point, most allow for adjustments to align with your brand.

2. **Custom Themes**
   - **Brand Consistency**: Tailor your theme to match your brand's unique identity.
   - **Flexibility**: Control every design aspect, from header styles to button colors.

Customizing Individual Elements

Beyond global settings, individual page elements such as buttons, banners, and menus can be tailored for a cohesive yet unique design.

1. **Buttons and CTAs**
   - **Color Contrast**: Ensure your buttons stand out with high contrast to encourage user interaction.
   - **Hover Effects**: Adding subtle animations enhances user engagement.

2. **Backgrounds and Images**
   - **Solid Colors vs. Patterns**: Choose a background style that complements your content without overwhelming it.
   - **Image Overlays**: Use semi-transparent layers to blend images with your color scheme.

Accessibility Considerations
Creating an inclusive website is crucial for reaching a broader audience.
1. **Contrast Ratios**
   - Ensure text is easily readable against background colors. Tools like WebAIM's contrast checker help evaluate compliance with accessibility standards.
2. **Color-Blind-Friendly Design**
   - Avoid relying solely on color to convey information. Use text labels or patterns alongside colors for clarity.

Testing and Refining Your Color Choices
Testing is an iterative process. A color scheme that looks great on a desktop may appear different on mobile devices or in varied lighting conditions.
1. **A/B Testing**
   - Experiment with different color combinations to see which drives better user engagement.
2. **User Feedback**
   - Collect input from real users to refine your color choices further.

Leveraging Analytics for Performance Insights
Once your color scheme is in place, use analytics tools to measure its impact. For instance, if your bounce rate is high, tweaking visual elements could improve user retention.

INTEGRATING IMAGES, VIDEOS, AND GRAPHICS

Importance of Visual Elements in Website Design

Visual elements play a crucial role in enhancing a website's appeal and effectiveness. They help communicate your brand's identity, improve user engagement, and convey complex information more effectively than text alone. In this section, we will explore how to seamlessly integrate images, videos, and graphics into your website to create a visually compelling experience.

Choosing the Right Visuals for Your Website

Selecting the appropriate visuals is the first step toward achieving a cohesive and professional design. Consider the following factors when choosing images, videos, and graphics:

- **Relevance**: Ensure that visuals align with your website's theme and content.
- **Quality**: Use high-resolution images and videos to maintain a professional appearance.
- **Consistency**: Stick to a consistent style, color palette, and tone across all visuals to reinforce your brand identity.

Optimizing Images for the Web

Large image files can slow down your website, negatively impacting user experience and SEO. Follow these best practices to optimize images:

- **File Formats**: Use JPEG for photos, PNG for images with transparency, and SVG for icons and logos.

- **Compression**: Utilize tools like TinyPNG or ImageOptim to reduce file sizes without compromising quality.

- **Responsive Design**: Ensure images adapt to various screen sizes by using responsive design techniques or platforms that support automatic resizing.

Embedding Videos for Enhanced Engagement

Videos are a powerful medium for storytelling and conveying complex information. Here's how to effectively integrate them:

- **Hosting Options**: Use platforms like YouTube or Vimeo for hosting to save bandwidth and ensure smooth playback.

- **Embedding Techniques**: Copy the embed code provided by the hosting platform and paste it into your website's code or editor.

- **Video Placement**: Position videos strategically on your site—such as on landing pages or product pages—to maximize their impact.

Utilizing Graphics to Communicate Ideas

Graphics, such as infographics, charts, and illustrations, help break down complex data and make your content more digestible. Here's how to use them effectively:

- **Create Custom Graphics**: Tools like Canva or

Adobe Illustrator enable you to design unique graphics tailored to your content.

- **Balance Text and Graphics**: Ensure that graphics complement the text rather than overwhelming it.
- **Interactive Elements**: Consider adding interactive graphics, such as clickable charts or animations, to increase user engagement.

Ensuring Accessibility in Visual Content

Making your website accessible to all users, including those with disabilities, is essential. Implement the following practices:

- **Alt Text for Images**: Provide descriptive alt text for images to assist users who rely on screen readers.
- **Captions and Transcripts for Videos**: Include captions or transcripts to make video content accessible to users with hearing impairments.
- **Readable Graphics**: Ensure that any text within graphics is legible and high-contrast.

Testing and Reviewing Visual Elements

After integrating visual elements, it's vital to test their performance and user impact:

- **Load Speed**: Use tools like Google PageSpeed Insights to check if visuals affect your website's loading time.
- **Responsiveness**: Verify that images and videos display correctly on various devices, including desktops, tablets, and smartphones.

- **User Feedback**: Collect feedback from visitors to determine whether your visuals enhance their experience or need adjustment.

CHAPTER 5: ENHANCING WEBSITE PERFORMANCE

Optimizing Load Times and Website Speed

Understanding the Importance of Website Speed

Website speed is a critical factor that directly impacts user experience, search engine rankings, and conversion rates. Studies show that users expect a webpage to load in under three seconds; any delay can result in higher bounce rates and lost opportunities. A fast-loading website keeps visitors engaged, boosts credibility, and enhances overall performance.

Factors Affecting Load Times

Several elements can influence how quickly your website loads. Identifying and optimizing these factors is essential for creating a seamless user experience:

1. **Large Images and Media Files**
    - High-resolution images and videos can significantly slow down your website. Compressing these files without compromising quality can dramatically improve speed.

2. **Unoptimized Code**
    - Bloated HTML, CSS, and JavaScript files increase load times. Minifying code by removing unnecessary characters and comments can streamline performance.

3. **Server Response Time**
   - The time it takes for your server to respond to user requests plays a crucial role. Choosing a reliable hosting provider ensures faster response times.
4. **Too Many Plugins or Widgets**
   - While plugins enhance functionality, excessive use can lead to slower performance. Regularly audit and remove unnecessary plugins.

Best Practices for Improving Load Times

1. Optimize Images and Media

- Use tools like TinyPNG or JPEG Optimizer to compress images. For videos, consider hosting them on platforms like YouTube or Vimeo and embedding them.
- Implement lazy loading, which ensures images only load when they appear on the user's screen.

2. Minify and Combine Files

- Minify your CSS, JavaScript, and HTML files to reduce their size. Tools like UglifyJS or CSSNano can automate this process.
- Combine multiple CSS or JavaScript files into one to reduce HTTP requests, enhancing speed.

3. Leverage Browser Caching

- Caching stores certain elements of your website on users' devices, reducing the time needed to load those elements on subsequent visits. Configure browser caching using .htaccess files or through your hosting provider.

4. Use a Content Delivery Network (CDN)

- A CDN distributes your website's content across multiple servers globally. This ensures users access data from the nearest server, speeding up load times. Services like Cloudflare or Amazon CloudFront are popular options.

5. Enable Gzip Compression

- Gzip reduces the size of your website's files before sending them to the user's browser, improving speed. Most modern servers support Gzip, and it can be activated through your hosting panel.

Monitoring Website Performance

Regular monitoring helps you stay ahead of potential performance issues. Use tools like:

- **Google PageSpeed Insights**: Offers suggestions for improving both desktop and mobile load times.
- **GTmetrix**: Provides detailed performance reports, including speed, structure, and waterfall charts.
- **Pingdom Tools**: Tests load times from various global locations.

These tools offer actionable insights, allowing you to track improvements and identify bottlenecks.

Optimizing for Mobile Speed

With the rise in mobile browsing, ensuring fast load

times on smartphones and tablets is paramount.

- **Adopt a Mobile-First Design**: Simplify your design for smaller screens to reduce load times.
- **Accelerated Mobile Pages (AMP)**: Use AMP to create lightweight pages that load instantly on mobile devices.
- **Responsive Images**: Use image formats like WebP, designed for faster loading on mobile devices.

The Role of Web Hosting in Speed Optimization

The hosting provider you choose can have a significant impact on your website's speed. Consider the following factors:

- **Server Location**: Select a hosting provider with servers close to your primary audience.
- **Type of Hosting**: Shared hosting can slow down your site during peak traffic. Upgrading to VPS or dedicated hosting offers better performance.
- **Built-in Speed Features**: Look for hosting providers that offer built-in caching, CDN integration, and Gzip compression.

Advanced Techniques for Speed Enhancement

For users comfortable with advanced configurations:

- **Asynchronous Loading of JavaScript**: This technique ensures scripts load independently, preventing slow elements from affecting overall speed.
- **Database Optimization**: Clean up and

optimize your website's database by removing unnecessary data and revising queries. Tools like WP-Optimize (for WordPress) can assist.

- **Prefetching and Preloading**: These techniques load resources in advance, improving perceived speed for users.

ENSURING MOBILE COMPATIBILITY AND RESPONSIVENESS

Understanding the Importance of Mobile Compatibility

In today's digital landscape, mobile devices account for a significant portion of web traffic. Ensuring your website is mobile-compatible is no longer optional; it's a necessity. Websites that are not optimized for mobile devices risk losing visitors and potential customers due to poor user experiences. Mobile compatibility means that your website not only displays correctly on smaller screens but also maintains full functionality.

Key Elements of a Mobile-Responsive Website

1. **Flexible Layouts**: A responsive design adjusts to various screen sizes and orientations. Whether your visitor is using a smartphone, tablet, or desktop, the website's layout should automatically reformat to provide the best viewing experience.

2. **Scalable Images and Media**: Images should resize proportionally to fit different screen sizes without compromising quality. Additionally, media like videos and slideshows must remain accessible and visually appealing on mobile devices.

3. **Touch-Friendly Navigation**: Mobile users rely on touch-based interactions. Buttons, links, and menus should be easily tappable, with enough spacing to prevent accidental clicks.
4. **Readable Text**: Font sizes should adjust dynamically for readability on smaller screens, eliminating the need for users to zoom in.

Using Built-in Tools for Mobile Optimization

Modern website builders provide robust tools for mobile optimization. These tools often include:

- **Mobile Preview Modes**: Allow you to see how your website will look on various devices.
- **Auto-Responsive Themes**: Pre-designed templates that are already optimized for mobile viewing.
- **Customizable Breakpoints**: Let you define how your website should behave at different screen widths.

Testing and Validating Mobile Compatibility

Testing your website across multiple devices is crucial for ensuring consistency. Here are some effective methods:

1. **Browser Developer Tools**: Most web browsers offer built-in developer tools that simulate various screen sizes and devices.
2. **Online Responsiveness Checkers**: Tools like Google's Mobile-Friendly Test provide detailed insights into your website's mobile compatibility.
3. **Physical Device Testing**: Whenever possible,

test your site on real devices to get a hands-on understanding of its performance.

Optimizing Performance for Mobile Users

Performance is a critical factor for mobile websites, as users on mobile devices often face slower internet speeds. Key areas to focus on include:

- **Minimizing Load Times**: Use optimized images, enable browser caching, and compress files to reduce load times.
- **Reducing Redirects**: Limit the number of redirects, as each one adds to the page load time.
- **Optimizing Code**: Minify CSS, JavaScript, and HTML to improve performance.

Best Practices for Mobile-First Design

A mobile-first approach prioritizes designing for mobile devices before scaling up for desktops. This methodology ensures that your website provides an optimal user experience on the most commonly used devices. Key strategies include:

- **Prioritizing Content**: Focus on essential content and functionality for mobile users.
- **Streamlined Navigation**: Use collapsible menus or hamburger icons to save screen space.
- **Avoiding Intrusive Elements**: Pop-ups and large ads can disrupt the user experience on mobile devices.

Common Pitfalls to Avoid

1. **Overloading Pages with Content**: Excessive

elements can slow down load times and overwhelm users.

2. **Neglecting Testing**: Failing to test across various devices can result in inconsistent user experiences.

3. **Ignoring Mobile SEO**: Mobile compatibility is a ranking factor for search engines. Ensure that your site adheres to mobile SEO best practices.

Leveraging Analytics for Continuous Improvement

Use analytics tools to monitor user behavior on mobile devices. Key metrics to track include:

- **Bounce Rate**: High bounce rates on mobile pages could indicate usability issues.

- **Session Duration**: Short sessions may suggest that users are struggling to engage with the content.

- **Conversion Rates**: Measure how effectively mobile visitors complete desired actions, such as filling out forms or making purchases.

MONITORING UPTIME AND WEBSITE SECURITY

website performance is a critical factor for user satisfaction and business success. Two key components of optimal performance are monitoring uptime and ensuring website security. Uptime monitoring helps maintain the availability of your site, while robust security measures protect your data and users from cyber threats.

Understanding Uptime and Its Importance

What Is Uptime?

Uptime refers to the amount of time a website is available and operational. It is typically expressed as a percentage, with "100% uptime" indicating uninterrupted availability. High uptime ensures that users can access your site whenever they need, enhancing their experience and trust.

Why Uptime Matters

1. **User Experience**: A website that frequently goes offline frustrates users and drives them away.

2. **SEO Impact**: Search engines like Google penalize websites with frequent downtimes, lowering their rankings.

3. **Revenue Loss**: For e-commerce sites, even a few minutes of downtime can lead to significant revenue losses.

Tools for Monitoring Uptime

Uptime Monitoring Services

Numerous tools help track your website's uptime, alerting you instantly if it goes down. Popular options include:

- **Pingdom**: Provides real-time alerts and performance reports.
- **UptimeRobot**: Offers free monitoring for up to 50 websites.
- **Site24x7**: Combines uptime monitoring with other performance analytics.

Implementing Automated Alerts

Set up automated alerts via email, SMS, or push notifications to get real-time updates on your website's status. This ensures quick action in case of an outage.

Website Security Essentials

Common Security Threats

1. **DDoS Attacks**: Overwhelm your server with traffic, causing downtime.
2. **Malware and Viruses**: Harm your site and compromise user data.
3. **Phishing and Social Engineering**: Trick users into revealing sensitive information.

Key Security Measures

1. Use SSL Certificates

SSL (Secure Sockets Layer) encrypts data transferred between the website and its users, ensuring sensitive information like passwords and credit card details remain secure. Websites with SSL certificates also gain a trust boost with the "https" prefix and a padlock icon in the address bar.

2. Regular Software Updates
Ensure that your website platform, plugins, and themes are up to date. Developers frequently release updates to patch security vulnerabilities.

3. Implement Firewalls
Web application firewalls (WAFs) protect your site from various attacks by filtering malicious traffic. They act as a barrier between your website and potential threats.

4. Secure Password Policies
Encourage strong passwords for user accounts, and implement multi-factor authentication (MFA) to add an extra layer of security.

Monitoring Website Security

Security Plugins and Tools

- **Sucuri Security**: Offers malware scanning and firewall protection.
- **Wordfence**: Provides comprehensive security solutions for WordPress sites.
- **Cloudflare**: Enhances both performance and security by mitigating DDoS attacks and offering content delivery network (CDN) services.

Conduct Regular Security Audits
Periodically review your website's security posture. This includes checking for outdated software, scanning for malware, and testing for vulnerabilities.

Backup Strategies

Maintain regular backups of your website to ensure data recovery in case of a security breach. Store these backups on secure, off-site locations or cloud services.

CHAPTER 6: BUILDING AN E-COMMERCE STORE

Setting Up Product Pages and Categories

A robust e-commerce store relies on well-structured product pages and logical categories. These components play a pivotal role in enhancing user experience and ensuring smooth navigation, ultimately driving sales. Setting them up correctly requires a balance of technical setup and strategic planning.

Understanding the Importance of Product Pages and Categories

A product page serves as the digital storefront for individual items. It must provide all relevant information, including product descriptions, images, pricing, and availability. Categories, on the other hand, organize products into logical groups, making it easier for customers to find what they need. Together, they form the foundation of a seamless shopping experience.

- **Boosting SEO:** Properly categorized products improve search engine rankings, increasing visibility.

- **Enhancing User Experience:** Clear categories and detailed product pages reduce bounce rates and improve customer satisfaction.

- **Facilitating Inventory Management:** Organized categories simplify stock tracking and updates.

Best Practices for Setting Up Product Pages

1. **Compelling Product Titles:** Use descriptive and keyword-rich titles to help customers and search engines understand your offerings.

2. **High-Quality Images:** Visuals significantly influence purchasing decisions. Include multiple high-resolution images, showcasing products from various angles.

3. **Detailed Descriptions:** Write concise but informative descriptions. Highlight key features, benefits, and specifications.

4. **Pricing and Promotions:** Display clear pricing, including discounts or special offers, to entice buyers.

5. **Customer Reviews and Ratings:** Enable customer reviews to build trust and provide social proof.

6. **Related Products and Upselling:** Recommend complementary or upgraded items to increase cart value.

Creating Effective Product Categories

1. **Logical Grouping:** Start by analyzing your inventory and segmenting it into broad categories, such as "Clothing," "Electronics," or "Home Decor." Break these down further into subcategories like "Men's T-Shirts" or "Smartphones."

2. **Intuitive Naming:** Use names that are familiar to your target audience. Avoid jargon or overly technical terms.

3. **Consistent Hierarchy:** Maintain a consistent structure across categories. Ensure each product fits into only one logical category to prevent redundancy.
4. **Search and Filter Options:** Enhance navigation with filters for price, brand, size, or color. This feature significantly improves the user experience.
5. **SEO Optimization for Categories:** Include keywords in category names and descriptions to improve search engine rankings.

Technical Setup for Product Pages and Categories

1. **Using Built-in E-Commerce Tools:** Many website builders offer e-commerce modules with pre-designed templates for product pages and categories. Customize these templates to align with your branding.
2. **Configuring Inventory Management:** Integrate inventory management tools to sync product availability across all pages automatically.
3. **Setting Up SKU and Product Codes:** Assign unique identifiers for each product to streamline tracking and reporting.
4. **Optimizing Load Times:** Use compressed images and efficient coding practices to ensure fast loading product pages, crucial for user retention.

Testing and Iterating for Success

1. **A/B Testing:** Experiment with different layouts, descriptions, or images to determine what

resonates best with your audience.

2. **Customer Feedback:** Encourage users to provide feedback on product pages and categories. Use this data to refine the design and content.

3. **Regular Updates:** Keep product information, pricing, and categories up-to-date to maintain relevance and accuracy.

CONFIGURING PAYMENT GATEWAYS AND CURRENCIES

What Are Payment Gateways?

Payment gateways are essential tools that allow businesses to process online transactions securely. They serve as intermediaries between a customer's bank and the merchant, ensuring that payment information is transmitted securely and efficiently.

Importance of Choosing the Right Gateway

Selecting the right payment gateway can significantly impact user experience and business operations. Key considerations include transaction fees, supported payment methods, and integration ease.

Popular Payment Gateway Options

1. **PayPal**: Widely recognized and trusted by consumers globally.

2. **Stripe**: Known for its developer-friendly API and flexible payment options.

3. **Square**: Ideal for businesses that also operate in physical locations.

4. **Authorize.Net**: Offers robust features for established businesses.

Setting Up Payment Gateways

Step 1: Evaluate Business Needs

Determine the types of payments you will accept (credit cards, digital wallets, etc.), transaction volume, and the geographic regions of your customers.

Step 2: Account Creation and Verification

Once you choose a gateway, you'll need to create an account. Most providers require verification documents, including business registration and banking details, to ensure compliance with financial regulations.

Step 3: Integration with the Website

Integration can typically be achieved through:

- **Built-in integrations**: Many website builders offer direct integration options.
- **APIs and Plugins**: For those requiring custom solutions, APIs and plugins provide greater flexibility.

Step 4: Testing Transactions

Before going live, run test transactions to ensure the gateway functions correctly and provides a seamless user experience.

Understanding and Configuring Currencies

Why Offer Multiple Currencies?

For businesses with international customers, offering multiple currencies enhances customer experience by eliminating the need for currency conversion during checkout.

Enabling Multi-Currency Support

Many platforms allow businesses to display prices in different currencies. This can be configured in the payment gateway or through additional plugins.

Currency Conversion Considerations

- **Exchange Rates**: Ensure that your platform updates exchange rates frequently.
- **Fees and Margins**: Be transparent about any fees added for currency conversion.

Best Practices for Payment and Currency Management

Ensure Security and Compliance

Secure payment gateways help protect sensitive customer data. Look for features like encryption and fraud detection. Additionally, ensure compliance with legal regulations like PCI DSS (Payment Card Industry Data Security Standard).

Offer Flexible Payment Options

Providing multiple payment methods, including credit/debit cards, digital wallets (like Apple Pay or Google Pay), and even Buy Now, Pay Later (BNPL) options, caters to a broader audience.

Monitor Payment Performance

Regularly review payment gateway performance metrics, including transaction success rates, processing times, and customer feedback.

Optimize for Mobile

Given the growing number of mobile shoppers, ensure your payment process is seamless on all devices.

Overcoming Common Challenges

High Transaction Fees

Some gateways charge significant fees for each transaction. Consider negotiating with providers or choosing a gateway with lower fees.

Currency Conversion Discrepancies

Automated systems sometimes apply outdated rates. Regularly check and update your system to ensure accuracy.

Integration Issues
If the payment gateway doesn't integrate smoothly, consult your platform's support team or hire a developer to resolve the issue promptly.

MANAGING INVENTORY AND ORDER FULFILLMENT

Inventory management is a cornerstone of any successful e-commerce store. Whether you sell physical products or digital goods, maintaining a well-organized inventory ensures smooth operations. Accurate inventory tracking helps prevent overselling, reduces holding costs, and improves customer satisfaction by minimizing delays in order fulfillment.

For e-commerce stores, inventory management involves several layers, including stock tracking, forecasting demand, and managing supplier relationships. Each of these aspects plays a critical role in ensuring that your store operates efficiently, even as it scales.

Key Elements of Inventory Management

1. **Real-Time Stock Tracking**
   Real-time stock tracking ensures you always have an accurate count of available products. Many e-commerce platforms, including Wix, offer integrated tools that automatically update inventory levels as orders are placed. This prevents overselling and eliminates the need for manual updates.

2. **Demand Forecasting**
   Demand forecasting uses historical data,

seasonal trends, and market analysis to predict future sales. This helps in planning stock purchases, ensuring you have enough inventory to meet demand without overstocking.

3. **Supplier Management**
   Building strong relationships with suppliers is essential. Reliable suppliers ensure timely delivery of stock, which directly impacts your ability to fulfill customer orders on time.

Order Fulfillment: Ensuring a Seamless Customer Experience

Order fulfillment is the process of receiving, processing, and delivering orders to customers. It includes several stages, each of which must be optimized for efficiency and accuracy.

1. **Order Processing**
   Once an order is placed, the system should automatically confirm stock availability and send an acknowledgment to the customer. This builds trust and sets clear expectations.

2. **Picking and Packing**
   Picking involves selecting the right products from your inventory. Packing ensures that the products are safely and securely prepared for shipping. Using standardized packing materials reduces costs and enhances the unboxing experience for customers.

3. **Shipping and Delivery**
   Offering multiple shipping options, including express and standard delivery, caters to customer preferences. Partnering with reliable

carriers minimizes delays and enhances the overall shopping experience.

Automation in Inventory and Fulfillment

Automation plays a pivotal role in modern e-commerce operations. By automating routine tasks like stock updates, order processing, and shipping label generation, you can reduce human errors and save time. Tools like Wix eCommerce integrate seamlessly with third-party applications, enabling automation across the supply chain.

Implementing a Return Management System

Efficient return management is crucial for maintaining customer satisfaction. A clear return policy, easy-to-navigate return process, and prompt refund or exchange procedures demonstrate your commitment to customer service. Managing returned inventory effectively helps minimize losses and ensures that products in resalable condition are promptly restocked.

Monitoring Key Performance Indicators (KPIs)

To gauge the effectiveness of your inventory and fulfillment processes, regularly monitor relevant KPIs. Key metrics include:

- **Inventory Turnover Ratio:** Measures how frequently your inventory is sold and replaced over a specific period.
- **Order Accuracy Rate:** Indicates the percentage of orders fulfilled without errors.
- **Order Cycle Time:** Tracks the time taken from receiving an order to its delivery.

- **Return Rate:** Helps identify product or process issues that lead to higher returns.

Best Practices for Efficient Inventory and Fulfillment

1. **Set Reorder Points**
   Determine minimum stock levels for each product. When stock dips below this point, the system automatically triggers a reorder, ensuring you never run out of high-demand items.

2. **Regular Audits**
   Conduct regular inventory audits to verify the accuracy of stock levels. These can be full audits or cycle counts, which involve checking a subset of your inventory.

3. **Optimize Storage**
   Organize your warehouse or storage space efficiently. Group similar products together, label shelves clearly, and use storage solutions like bins or racks to maximize space.

4. **Provide Transparent Communication**
   Keep customers informed about their order status, including any delays. Transparent communication builds trust and reduces the likelihood of negative reviews.

Leveraging Technology for Continuous Improvement

Investing in technology can significantly enhance your inventory and fulfillment processes. Tools like predictive analytics help anticipate market trends, while advanced shipping software can optimize routes and reduce delivery times. Regularly review and upgrade your systems to stay competitive in a fast-paced e-commerce landscape.

CREATING A CUSTOMER-FRIENDLY CHECKOUT EXPERIENCE

Creating a seamless and user-friendly checkout experience is crucial for any e-commerce store. This stage in the shopping journey can significantly influence a customer's decision to complete a purchase. Below, we'll explore the key elements of designing a checkout process that enhances user satisfaction and boosts conversion rates.

The Importance of a Streamlined Checkout Process

The checkout process is the final step in converting website visitors into paying customers. A complex or lengthy checkout can lead to cart abandonment, negatively impacting sales. Studies show that a simplified, intuitive checkout experience can increase conversion rates by up to 35%.

Key Elements of an Effective Checkout Design

1. Guest Checkout Option

Not all customers want to create an account before making a purchase. Offering a guest checkout option removes this barrier, making the process quicker and more appealing for first-time buyers.

2. Minimal Form Fields

Request only the essential information required to

complete the transaction. Long forms can be off-putting and lead to abandonment. Focus on fields such as name, shipping address, and payment details.

3. Progress Indicators

A progress bar or step-by-step indicator reassures users by showing how far they've come and how much is left to complete the purchase. This feature can reduce anxiety and keep customers engaged.

Ensuring Payment Security and Transparency

1. Secure Payment Options

Highlight secure payment methods and display trust badges from reputable payment processors. This builds confidence in the safety of financial transactions.

2. Clear Pricing Breakdown

Customers appreciate transparency. Provide a detailed breakdown of costs, including product price, taxes, shipping fees, and any applicable discounts, before they reach the payment page.

Reducing Cart Abandonment

1. Save Cart Feature

Allow users to save their cart for later. This is particularly useful for customers who may not be ready to complete their purchase immediately but intend to return.

2. Exit-Intent Popups

When users attempt to leave the checkout page, a well-timed popup offering a discount or free shipping can entice them to stay and complete their purchase.

3. Multiple Payment Methods

Provide diverse payment options, including credit cards, PayPal, and other region-specific methods. This caters to a broader audience and increases the likelihood of successful transactions.

Mobile Optimization for Checkout

Mobile commerce continues to grow, making it essential to optimize the checkout process for smaller screens. Features such as autofill for addresses, mobile-friendly payment options like Apple Pay or Google Pay, and touch-friendly buttons can enhance the mobile user experience.

Post-Purchase Features

1. Order Confirmation

Immediately after the purchase, provide a confirmation page and email summarizing the order details. This reassures customers that their order was successful.

2. Easy Returns and Refunds

Clearly outline your return and refund policies on the checkout page. A hassle-free return process builds trust and encourages repeat business.

Leveraging Customer Feedback

After checkout, encourage customers to provide feedback about their experience. Use this data to identify pain points and make continuous improvements to your checkout process.

CHAPTER 7: ADVANCED WEBSITE FEATURES

Incorporating Social Media Integrations

Why Social Media Integration Matters

Social media platforms have become an essential component of online marketing strategies. Integrating these platforms into your website is crucial for engaging visitors, driving traffic, and building brand awareness. Whether you are running a personal blog or a business site, social media integration helps establish a dynamic and interactive presence.

Types of Social Media Integrations

1. Social Sharing Buttons

Adding social sharing buttons to your website allows visitors to share your content directly on their social media profiles. These buttons are typically placed on blog posts, product pages, and other shareable content. They help increase your site's visibility and attract more traffic.

2. Social Media Feeds

Embedding live feeds from platforms like Instagram, Twitter, or Facebook showcases your latest posts directly on your website. This not only keeps your site updated with fresh content but also encourages visitors to follow your social accounts.

3. Login via Social Media

Offering social media login options simplifies the

user registration process. Visitors can sign in using their existing social media accounts, enhancing user convenience and reducing barriers to engagement.

4. Social Media Widgets and Plugins
Widgets like Facebook Messenger or WhatsApp Chat enable real-time communication between you and your audience. These tools are valuable for customer support, providing quick responses to inquiries and enhancing user experience.

Best Practices for Social Media Integration

1. Prioritize Platforms Relevant to Your Audience
Not all social media platforms will be relevant to your target audience. Focus on the platforms where your audience is most active. For example, visual platforms like Instagram and Pinterest work well for lifestyle and fashion brands, while LinkedIn is ideal for B2B companies.

2. Maintain Visual Consistency
Ensure that social media elements, such as buttons and widgets, match your website's design and branding. Consistency in color schemes, fonts, and overall layout creates a cohesive user experience.

3. Optimize for Mobile Devices
With a significant portion of web traffic coming from mobile devices, ensure that your social media integrations are mobile-friendly. Test your site's responsiveness to guarantee seamless functionality across various screen sizes.

4. Monitor Performance and Engagement
Use analytics tools to track how visitors interact with your social media integrations. Identify which platforms

drive the most traffic and engagement, and adjust your strategy accordingly.

Implementing Social Media Integrations

Step 1: Choose the Right Tools

Most website builders and content management systems offer built-in tools or plugins for social media integration. Explore options that align with your site's goals and functionality.

Step 2: Configure and Customize

Once you've selected the tools, configure them according to your needs. Customize the appearance and placement of social sharing buttons, feeds, and widgets to align with your website design.

Step 3: Test Functionality

Before launching your site, thoroughly test each integration to ensure proper functionality. Check for broken links, loading issues, and responsiveness.

Step 4: Encourage Social Engagement

Promote your social media presence by encouraging visitors to follow your accounts. Consider offering incentives, such as exclusive content or discounts, to those who engage with your social profiles.

Benefits of Social Media Integration

1. **Enhanced User Engagement**: Social media interactions foster a sense of community and keep your audience engaged.
2. **Increased Website Traffic**: Shared content on social platforms can drive more visitors to your site.
3. **Improved SEO**: Social signals, such as shares and

likes, can indirectly boost your website's search engine ranking.

4. **Streamlined Communication**: Real-time messaging tools improve customer support and foster stronger relationships with your audience.

Avoiding Common Pitfalls

1. **Overloading Your Site**
Avoid cluttering your website with excessive social media widgets and plugins, as this can slow down load times and overwhelm visitors.

2. **Ignoring Privacy Concerns**
Be transparent about data usage, especially if you implement social login options. Ensure compliance with data protection regulations like GDPR.

3. **Neglecting Updates**
Social media platforms frequently update their APIs, which can impact the functionality of your integrations. Regularly update your tools to avoid disruptions.

4. **Overemphasis on Vanity Metrics**
While likes and shares are important, focus on meaningful engagement metrics, such as comments and click-through rates, to gauge the effectiveness of your social strategy.

UTILIZING WIDGETS AND PLUGINS FOR EXTENDED FUNCTIONALITY

Widgets and plugins are essential tools for enhancing the functionality and user experience of your website. While a website's core structure provides the framework, these tools allow you to extend capabilities, add features, and improve the overall user interface without needing to dive into complex coding.

Understanding the Role of Widgets and Plugins

Widgets are pre-built modules that provide specific functions, such as displaying recent posts, showing weather updates, or integrating social media feeds. Plugins, on the other hand, are software add-ons that enhance or expand the functionality of your website's platform. Together, they allow users to incorporate dynamic features, improve website interactivity, and optimize the site's performance.

Categories of Widgets and Plugins

To ensure optimal functionality, it's essential to understand the different categories available:

1. **Content Widgets**: Display recent posts, galleries, or user testimonials.

2. **Social Media Integrations**: Embed feeds or sharing buttons from platforms like Instagram, Twitter, or Facebook.

3. **Performance Optimization Plugins**: Tools like caching plugins that enhance site speed.
4. **E-commerce Plugins**: Enable product listings, shopping carts, and payment gateways.
5. **SEO Widgets and Plugins**: Improve your website's visibility on search engines by optimizing metadata and content.

Benefits of Using Widgets and Plugins

- **Enhanced User Experience**: Add interactive and engaging features like forms, sliders, and real-time chat.
- **Increased Functionality**: Go beyond basic site setups by adding e-commerce capabilities, event calendars, or customer portals.
- **Customization Flexibility**: Tailor your website to meet specific needs without altering the main code.
- **Improved Performance**: Some plugins help in compressing images or optimizing scripts for faster load times.

Selecting the Right Tools

The effectiveness of widgets and plugins depends on selecting the right ones. Consider these factors:

- **Compatibility**: Ensure that the tool works seamlessly with your platform and theme.
- **Reviews and Ratings**: Opt for plugins with high ratings and positive user feedback.
- **Support and Updates**: Choose tools that are

regularly updated and supported to avoid security vulnerabilities.

- **Ease of Use**: Especially important for beginners; prioritize user-friendly tools with intuitive interfaces.

Popular Widgets and Plugins for Extended Functionality

1. **Yoast SEO**: Helps in optimizing content for search engines.
2. **WooCommerce**: Ideal for building an online store.
3. **Contact Form 7**: Simplifies adding custom forms for user inquiries.
4. **Slider Revolution**: Adds visually appealing sliders and carousels.
5. **Jetpack**: Offers a suite of tools for site performance, security, and design.

Best Practices for Installing and Managing Plugins

- **Limit the Number of Plugins**: Too many can slow down your website and cause compatibility issues.
- **Regular Updates**: Ensure plugins are updated to their latest versions to maintain functionality and security.
- **Backup Before Installation**: Protect your website's data by creating backups before adding or updating plugins.
- **Test for Conflicts**: After installing a new plugin,

check your site for any unexpected issues or performance drops.

Troubleshooting Common Issues with Widgets and Plugins

1. **Website Slows Down**: Deactivate unnecessary plugins and use performance optimization tools.
2. **Plugin Conflicts**: Resolve issues by deactivating plugins one by one to identify the source of the problem.
3. **Security Vulnerabilities**: Use plugins from reputable sources and always keep them updated.
4. **Broken Features After Updates**: Roll back to previous versions while reporting the issue to the developer.

CREATING MEMBERSHIP AREAS AND SUBSCRIPTION SERVICES

Understanding Membership and Subscription Models

Creating membership areas and subscription services is an excellent way to offer exclusive content, foster community, and generate recurring revenue. Membership models allow website owners to segment their audience, offering different levels of access based on user subscriptions. These features are especially useful for businesses, educators, and content creators who want to monetize their expertise or provide tiered content access.

Membership areas typically include forums, exclusive blogs, downloadable content, and special event access. Subscription services, on the other hand, might involve regular product deliveries, online courses, or premium features in a SaaS (Software as a Service) platform.

Benefits of Membership and Subscription Services

1. **Recurring Revenue Streams:** Unlike one-time purchases, subscriptions provide predictable and steady income.
2. **User Retention and Loyalty:** Exclusive content encourages users to stay engaged and renew their subscriptions.

3. **Data Collection and Personalization:** Memberships allow for better user data collection, enabling personalized content and marketing.

4. **Community Building:** Membership platforms often foster a sense of belonging, strengthening the bond between users and the brand.

Setting Up Membership Areas

1. **Define Your Membership Levels:**
   Decide on the types of memberships you'll offer. Will there be free access levels, or will all tiers require payment? Clearly define the benefits of each level.

2. **Secure Login and Registration Systems:**
   Ensure a seamless registration process with secure login credentials. Use tools or plugins that allow easy account management and password recovery.

3. **Designing the Membership Dashboard:**
   A well-designed dashboard enhances user experience. Members should easily access their content, manage subscriptions, and interact with the community.

4. **Content Access Controls:**
   Use permissions to control which content is accessible to different membership levels. For example, premium members might access new articles or videos before standard members.

Implementing Subscription Services

1. **Choosing a Payment Gateway:**
   Select a payment gateway that supports recurring billing. Popular options include PayPal, Stripe, and Authorize.net. Ensure that your choice aligns with your target audience's preferences and offers secure transactions.

2. **Setting Up Pricing Plans:**
   Offer flexible pricing plans to cater to a wider audience. Monthly, quarterly, and annual subscriptions often appeal to different customer segments.

3. **Automated Billing and Renewal Notifications:**
   Implement systems that automatically charge users at the end of each billing cycle and notify them of upcoming renewals. This reduces churn and improves customer satisfaction.

4. **Offering Free Trials and Discounts:**
   Attract potential subscribers with limited-time free trials or introductory discounts. These strategies help users experience your service risk-free, increasing conversion rates.

Tools and Plugins for Membership and Subscription Management

To create efficient membership and subscription systems, leverage the following tools:

1. **MemberSpace** – A versatile tool for adding membership functionality without coding.

2. **Paid Memberships Pro** – Ideal for setting up tiered memberships and integrating with payment gateways.

3. **Sentry Login** – Provides robust security for membership sites.

4. **Stripe Subscriptions** – A seamless way to handle recurring payments with extensive customization options.

5. **WooCommerce Subscriptions** – Perfect for e-commerce platforms needing subscription models.

Ensuring Security and Compliance

User data security is paramount in any membership or subscription service.

1. **Data Encryption:** Ensure that sensitive information, such as credit card details, is encrypted.

2. **GDPR and CCPA Compliance:** Be transparent about data collection and use. Provide easy ways for users to manage their data and privacy preferences.

3. **Regular Security Audits:** Conduct audits to identify vulnerabilities and address them promptly.

Enhancing User Experience

1. **Mobile Compatibility:** Many users access membership content on mobile devices. Ensure your platform is fully responsive.

2. **Support and Communication Channels:** Offer robust customer support through live chat, FAQs, or ticket systems. Keep members updated with newsletters and in-platform notifications.

3. **Gamification and Incentives:** Enhance

engagement by incorporating badges, leaderboards, or other gamified elements to reward active members.

Monitoring Performance and Feedback

1. **Track Key Metrics:** Monitor metrics such as churn rate, average revenue per user (ARPU), and user engagement levels.
2. **User Feedback:** Regularly seek member feedback to identify areas for improvement. Conduct surveys and polls or allow direct feedback via your platform.

Growing and Scaling Membership Services

As your membership base grows, consider expanding your offerings:

- **Collaborations:** Partner with other businesses to provide additional value to members.
- **New Content Types:** Introduce webinars, podcasts, or exclusive virtual events.
- **Tiered Expansions:** Offer higher-tier memberships with exclusive perks as demand grows.

CHAPTER 8: SEARCH ENGINE OPTIMIZATION (SEO) BASICS

Understanding SEO and Its Importance

Search Engine Optimization (SEO) is a vital component of online visibility. At its core, SEO involves optimizing a website to rank higher in search engine results, making it more accessible to potential visitors. Whether you're a small business owner, a content creator, or running an e-commerce store, understanding SEO can significantly impact your online success.

The Role of Search Engines in Online Visibility

Search engines like Google, Bing, and Yahoo serve as the primary gateway for users seeking information online. They use complex algorithms to evaluate websites and determine their relevance to specific queries. By optimizing your site according to these algorithms, you increase its chances of appearing at the top of search results.

Key Benefits of SEO

1. **Increased Website Traffic**
   SEO brings organic traffic, which refers to visitors who find your site through unpaid search results. Unlike paid advertising, organic traffic is cost-effective and often more sustainable in the long run.

2. **Improved User Experience**
   SEO isn't just about search engines; it's about improving the user experience as well. By focusing on elements like site speed, mobile compatibility, and quality content, you ensure that visitors have a seamless experience.

3. **Higher Credibility and Trust**
   Websites that appear at the top of search results are often perceived as more credible and trustworthy. Effective SEO helps establish your authority in your niche, fostering trust among your audience.

4. **Better Conversion Rates**
   Targeted SEO ensures that you attract visitors genuinely interested in your products or services, which increases the likelihood of conversions, whether that's a purchase, a sign-up, or any other desired action.

Core Components of SEO

1. **On-Page SEO**
   This involves optimizing individual pages to rank higher. Key elements include:
   - **Title Tags and Meta Descriptions**: These elements summarize your content and appear in search results, influencing click-through rates.
   - **Keywords**: Researching and strategically placing relevant keywords in your content helps search engines understand your page's focus.
   - **Content Quality**: Creating high-value,

original content is crucial for engaging users and keeping them on your site.

- **URL Structure**: Clean and descriptive URLs enhance usability and make it easier for search engines to index your pages.

2. **Technical SEO**

   Technical SEO focuses on the backend elements of your website:
   - **Site Speed**: A fast-loading website improves user experience and reduces bounce rates.
   - **Mobile Optimization**: With the majority of web traffic coming from mobile devices, ensuring your site is mobile-friendly is essential.
   - **XML Sitemaps**: These help search engines understand the structure of your website and index it effectively.

3. **Off-Page SEO**

   Off-page SEO revolves around activities outside your website:
   - **Backlinking**: Gaining links from reputable websites enhances your site's authority.
   - **Social Signals**: Engaging on social media can drive traffic and signal relevance to search engines.

4. **Local SEO**

   For businesses with a physical presence, local SEO ensures you appear in location-based searches. This includes optimizing your Google My Business profile and earning positive reviews.

SEO Tools and Resources

Several tools can help streamline your SEO efforts:

- **Google Analytics**: Tracks website traffic and user behavior.
- **Google Search Console**: Provides insights into your website's performance in search results.
- **Keyword Research Tools**: Tools like SEMrush or Ahrefs help identify high-value keywords.

Common SEO Mistakes to Avoid

1. **Keyword Stuffing**
   Overloading your content with keywords can lead to penalties and diminish user experience.

2. **Ignoring Mobile Optimization**
   Search engines prioritize mobile-friendly sites, so neglecting this aspect can hurt your rankings.

3. **Neglecting Analytics**
   Without analyzing your site's performance, it's difficult to gauge the effectiveness of your SEO strategies.

OPTIMIZING CONTENT AND META TAGS

Search engines prioritize high-quality, relevant, and user-friendly content. To rank well, your website must offer value to visitors by answering their queries, addressing their needs, or solving their problems. Well-optimized content not only improves your ranking but also enhances user experience.

- **Relevance**: Content should align with users' search intent. Identify the common questions your audience asks and craft content to address those topics.

- **Keyword Strategy**: Incorporate relevant keywords naturally within your content. Use tools like Google Keyword Planner to identify terms with high search volume and manageable competition.

- **Content Length and Depth**: Search engines favor comprehensive content. Articles, blogs, and guides exceeding 1,000 words often perform better in search rankings. However, always prioritize quality over quantity.

Crafting Engaging Meta Titles and Descriptions

Meta titles and descriptions are crucial for driving click-through rates (CTR) from search engine results pages (SERPs). These elements provide a snapshot of your page's content to users and search engines.

- **Meta Titles**:
    - Include primary keywords at the beginning of the title.
    - Limit titles to 50-60 characters to prevent truncation in SERPs.
    - Ensure titles are compelling and accurately reflect the page content.
- **Meta Descriptions**:
    - Use 150-160 characters to summarize the page's content effectively.
    - Incorporate secondary keywords naturally.
    - Include a call-to-action (CTA) to encourage clicks (e.g., "Learn more," "Get started today").

Optimizing Header Tags (H1, H2, H3)

Header tags structure your content, improving readability and signaling importance to search engines.

- **H1 Tag**: This is the main title of your page. Ensure it includes your primary keyword and concisely conveys the topic.
- **H2 and H3 Tags**: These are used for subheadings. They should include related keywords to support the main topic and improve the content's SEO value.

Image Optimization

Images enhance content but can slow down page load times if not optimized. Search engines also rely on image metadata to understand the content better.

- **File Names**: Rename image files to describe their content using keywords (e.g., "product-image-blue-shirt.jpg").
- **Alt Text**: Provide descriptive alt text for all images, incorporating relevant keywords to improve accessibility and SEO.
- **Compression**: Use tools like TinyPNG to compress images without compromising quality, reducing load times.

Internal and External Linking

Links help search engines understand your website's structure and determine content relevance.

- **Internal Links**:
    - Link to other relevant pages within your website to keep users engaged.
    - Use descriptive anchor text to help users and search engines understand the linked page's content.
- **External Links**:
    - Cite authoritative sources to back up claims or provide additional context.
    - Ensure the links open in a new tab to keep users on your site.

Maintaining Content Freshness

Regularly updating your content signals search engines that your site remains relevant.

- **Content Audits**: Periodically review old content to update statistics, improve keyword usage, and correct outdated information.
- **Repurposing Content**: Transform high-performing blog posts into videos, infographics, or social media content.
- **User Engagement**: Encourage user comments and interactions to keep content dynamic and engaging.

Technical SEO Considerations for Content

While content is crucial, technical elements also play a role in optimizing it.

- **Canonical Tags**: Prevent duplicate content issues by using canonical tags to indicate the preferred version of a page.
- **Structured Data**: Implement schema markup to help search engines better understand your content and improve SERP visibility.

LEVERAGING WIX SEO TOOLS FOR BETTER RANKINGS

Search engine optimization (SEO) is critical for ensuring your website reaches its target audience. Wix offers a suite of built-in SEO tools designed to help users optimize their websites effectively, regardless of technical expertise. This section will explore how to maximize these tools to boost your website's search engine rankings.

Understanding SEO Basics

Before diving into specific tools, it's essential to understand the fundamentals of SEO. At its core, SEO involves optimizing your website to rank higher in search engine results pages (SERPs). This process includes improving various elements such as content, keywords, meta descriptions, and backlinks.

Key Elements of SEO

- **Keywords:** The phrases potential visitors type into search engines.
- **Meta Tags:** Descriptive tags that provide search engines with information about your site.
- **Content Quality:** High-quality, relevant content keeps visitors engaged and improves SEO.
- **Backlinks:** Links from other reputable websites

that boost your site's authority.

- **Mobile Optimization:** Ensuring your site performs well on mobile devices is crucial for SEO.

Exploring Wix's SEO Tools

Wix provides several tools and features tailored to enhance your site's SEO. These tools make the process accessible, even for those with limited technical knowledge.

1. SEO Wiz

The SEO Wiz is an interactive tool that guides users through the optimization process. It generates a personalized SEO plan based on your website's specific goals.

- **Step-by-Step Guidance:** The Wiz walks you through tasks such as setting up meta tags, improving content, and optimizing images.
- **Progress Tracking:** It monitors your progress, highlighting areas that need improvement.

2. Meta Tags and Descriptions

Meta tags and descriptions are critical for providing search engines and users with concise information about your pages.

- **Customization Options:** Wix allows easy editing of title tags and meta descriptions for each page.
- **Preview Feature:** You can see how your pages will appear in search results, ensuring they are compelling and informative.

3. URL Customization

A clean and descriptive URL structure improves both user experience and SEO.

- **Editable URLs:** Wix lets you customize URLs to include relevant keywords.
- **Automatic Redirects:** If you update a URL, Wix automatically sets up a redirect to avoid broken links.

4. Alt Text for Images

Adding alt text to images enhances accessibility and helps search engines understand your content better.

- **User-Friendly Interface:** Wix simplifies the process of adding alt text, ensuring every image contributes to your SEO efforts.

Optimizing Content with Wix

Content is king in the SEO world, and Wix provides several tools to help you create and optimize high-quality content.

Content Manager

The Content Manager allows you to organize and display dynamic content easily.

- **Dynamic Pages:** Create pages that automatically pull content from your database.
- **SEO-Friendly Fields:** Ensure each dynamic page has unique meta tags and descriptions.

Blog Integration

A blog can significantly boost your SEO by providing fresh, relevant content.

- **Built-In Blog Platform:** Wix's blogging tools are easy to use and integrate seamlessly with your site.

- **SEO Features for Blogs:** Customize meta tags, URLs, and categories to improve your blog's visibility.

Advanced SEO Features

For users looking to take their SEO efforts further, Wix offers advanced features.

Structured Data Markup

Structured data helps search engines understand your content more effectively.

- **Built-In Support:** Wix allows you to add structured data to your site without needing to write code.

- **Enhanced SERP Features:** Implementing structured data can lead to rich snippets, such as star ratings or event times, making your site stand out in search results.

Canonical Tags

Canonical tags prevent duplicate content issues by specifying the preferred version of a page.

- **Easy Implementation:** Wix makes it simple to add canonical tags to your pages.

Analyzing Performance with Wix's SEO Tools

Monitoring and analyzing your SEO performance is crucial for continuous improvement.

SEO Reports

Wix generates regular SEO reports that provide insights into your website's performance.

- **Traffic Analysis:** Understand where your

visitors are coming from and which pages are most popular.

- **Keyword Rankings:** Track how your chosen keywords are performing in search results.

Integration with Google Analytics

For deeper insights, Wix integrates seamlessly with Google Analytics.

- **Behavior Tracking:** Analyze how visitors interact with your site.

- **Conversion Tracking:** Monitor how effectively your site converts visitors into customers or subscribers.

Best Practices for Using Wix SEO Tools

While Wix simplifies the SEO process, following best practices ensures you get the most out of its tools.

1. Regular Updates

Search engines favor sites that regularly update their content.

- **Fresh Content:** Keep your blog and pages updated with new, relevant information.

- **SEO Checkups:** Use the SEO Wiz periodically to identify areas for improvement.

2. Focus on User Experience

Good SEO is about more than just appeasing search engines; it's about providing value to users.

- **Fast Load Times:** Ensure your site loads quickly.

- **Mobile Responsiveness:** Your site should perform well on all devices.

3. Stay Informed

SEO is constantly evolving.

- **Industry Trends:** Stay updated on the latest SEO trends and algorithm changes.
- **Wix Updates:** Take advantage of new features as Wix continues to enhance its platform.

CHAPTER 9: ANALYTICS AND PERFORMANCE TRACKING

Setting Up Google Analytics

Google Analytics (GA) is a vital tool for anyone looking to optimize their website's performance. It provides detailed insights into user behavior, allowing you to make informed decisions to enhance user experience and achieve your business goals.

Why Google Analytics is Essential

Understanding how visitors interact with your website is crucial for growth. GA allows you to:

- **Monitor Traffic Sources**: Know where your visitors are coming from—whether through search engines, social media, or direct traffic.

- **Track User Behavior**: Identify which pages perform well and which need improvement.

- **Measure Conversions**: Analyze how effectively your website converts visitors into customers or leads.

- **Optimize Marketing Strategies**: Fine-tune your marketing efforts by tracking campaign performance.

Creating a Google Analytics Account

1. **Sign Up**: Visit the Google Analytics website and sign up with your Google account.
2. **Set Up a Property**: A property represents your website or app. Enter your website's name, URL, and industry category.
3. **Get Your Tracking ID**: GA provides a unique tracking code to be embedded in your website.

Integrating Google Analytics with Wix

1. **Accessing Your Wix Dashboard**: Log into your Wix account and open the dashboard for the site you want to track.
2. **Installing the Tracking Code**:
    - Navigate to **Settings > Tracking Tools & Analytics**.
    - Click **+ New Tool** and select **Google Analytics**.
    - Paste the tracking ID provided by GA.
3. **Verifying Integration**: Ensure GA is correctly installed by checking the "Real-Time" section in your GA dashboard after visiting your website.

Configuring Google Analytics Settings

1. **Account and Property Settings**: Customize data sharing settings and property details to match your business needs.
2. **Goals and Conversions**:
    - Set up goals such as form submissions,

purchases, or newsletter sign-ups.
- Assign values to these goals to measure their impact on your revenue.
3. **Filters**: Exclude internal traffic (e.g., your visits) to get accurate data.

Understanding the Google Analytics Dashboard

1. **Home**: A quick overview of key metrics, including user count, sessions, and bounce rate.
2. **Reports**:
   - **Audience**: Demographics, interests, and location data.
   - **Acquisition**: Insights into how users find your website.
   - **Behavior**: Data on user interaction with your site.
   - **Conversions**: Tracks goal completions and e-commerce transactions.

Leveraging Google Analytics Data

1. **Identifying Popular Content**: Determine which pages or posts engage users the most and replicate their success.
2. **Improving User Experience**:
   - Analyze bounce rates to identify pages where users lose interest.
   - Optimize navigation and content layout based on user behavior.
3. **Refining Marketing Campaigns**:
   - Evaluate the effectiveness of your SEO and PPC efforts.

- Focus on high-performing channels for better ROI.

Advanced Google Analytics Features

1. **Custom Dashboards**: Create personalized dashboards to track metrics relevant to your goals.
2. **Event Tracking**: Monitor specific actions like button clicks, video plays, or downloads.
3. **E-commerce Tracking**: For online stores, track sales, product performance, and customer behavior.

Common Mistakes to Avoid

1. **Ignoring Data Accuracy**: Ensure proper implementation of tracking code to avoid skewed data.
2. **Overlooking Mobile Analytics**: With a significant portion of web traffic coming from mobile devices, pay attention to mobile user data.
3. **Not Setting Goals**: Without goals, you won't measure what matters most to your business.

UNDERSTANDING KEY WEBSITE METRICS AND KPIS

Why Website Metrics and KPIs Matter

Metrics and Key Performance Indicators (KPIs) are the backbone of data-driven decision-making for any website. They provide insights into visitor behavior, assess performance, and inform improvements to meet business goals. Understanding these metrics is essential for optimizing your website's effectiveness.

Key Metrics Every Website Owner Should Monitor

1. **Traffic Volume**
   Traffic metrics quantify the number of visitors to your website. These include:
     - **Total Visitors**: The cumulative count of individuals accessing your site within a given period.
     - **Unique Visitors**: The number of distinct users visiting your website, each counted once regardless of frequency.

Why It Matters: A steady increase in traffic is a sign of growing interest and visibility, while declines could indicate issues with visibility or content relevance.

2. **Bounce Rate**
   The percentage of visitors who leave after

viewing only one page. A high bounce rate can suggest:
- Poor user experience.
- Irrelevant landing pages.
- Ineffective call-to-action (CTA) placement.

How to Improve: Optimize landing pages and ensure content matches visitor expectations.

3. **Average Session Duration**
   This metric measures the average time users spend on your site during a visit. A longer session typically indicates:
   - Engaging content.
   - A user-friendly design.

Enhancements: Include interactive features, relevant links, and engaging media to retain visitor attention.

Engagement Metrics: Tracking User Interaction

1. **Pages Per Session**
   This indicates how many pages a visitor views during a single session. It's a good measure of user engagement and content relevancy.

Strategies for Improvement: Use internal linking to encourage users to explore more pages and offer related content suggestions.

2. **Click-Through Rate (CTR)**
   CTR tracks the percentage of users who click on a specific link, often used in email campaigns or advertisements.

Importance: A high CTR implies that your content or ads are compelling and effective.

Conversion Metrics: Measuring Success

1. **Goal Completions**
   Also known as conversions, these are specific actions you want visitors to take, such as signing up for a newsletter, completing a purchase, or submitting a contact form.

Optimizing for Conversions: Ensure your calls-to-action are prominent and provide clear value propositions.

2. **Conversion Rate**
   This is the percentage of visitors who complete a desired action out of the total number of visitors. A high conversion rate indicates the effectiveness of your website's content and user journey.

Tips to Improve: Conduct A/B testing for CTAs, simplify navigation, and reduce form fields to minimize barriers.

Operational Metrics for Site Health

1. **Page Load Time**
   The time it takes for a webpage to fully load. Slow load times can lead to higher bounce rates and lower search engine rankings.

Action Steps: Compress images, enable browser caching, and minimize server response times.

2. **Uptime**
   Uptime measures the percentage of time your website is operational. High uptime ensures constant availability to users.

Monitoring Tools: Use services like UptimeRobot or Pingdom to track site performance.

Custom KPIs Based on Business Goals

Tailoring KPIs to your specific business objectives can help in tracking the most relevant data. Examples include:

- **E-commerce Sites**: Revenue per visitor, average order value, and cart abandonment rate.
- **Content Platforms**: Social shares, time spent on content, and returning visitor rate.
- **Service Providers**: Lead generation metrics like form submissions or inquiry calls.

How to Use Metrics for Continuous Improvement

1. **Set Baselines and Targets**
   Establishing a baseline helps in measuring progress over time. Define achievable targets to encourage incremental improvements.

2. **Analyze Trends Over Time**
   Don't rely solely on single data points. Trends reveal patterns, such as seasonality or shifts in user behavior.

3. **Use Insights to Optimize**
   Data from metrics and KPIs should guide changes. For instance:
   - High bounce rates? Redesign landing pages.
   - Low session durations? Reassess content engagement strategies.

ANALYZING USER BEHAVIOR AND TRAFFIC SOURCES

User behavior analysis is critical for optimizing website performance. By examining how users interact with a site—what pages they visit, how long they stay, and where they drop off—site owners can make informed decisions to improve user experience and achieve business goals.

Traffic Sources and Their Impact on Strategy

Traffic sources reveal where your website visitors come from, whether through organic search, paid ads, social media, or direct visits. Understanding these sources helps prioritize marketing efforts and allocate resources effectively. For example:

- **Organic Traffic**: Indicates success in search engine optimization (SEO).
- **Paid Traffic**: Shows the effectiveness of advertising campaigns.
- **Social Media Traffic**: Reflects audience engagement and content effectiveness on social platforms.

Tools for Analyzing User Behavior and Traffic

Several tools can help monitor and analyze user behavior and traffic sources:

- **Google Analytics**: Offers detailed insights into visitor demographics, behavior, and traffic sources.
- **Heatmaps**: Tools like Hotjar show where users click, scroll, and spend the most time on a page.
- **Session Recordings**: Replay user sessions to understand the journey and identify obstacles.

Key Metrics for Understanding User Behavior

Tracking the right metrics is essential for a comprehensive analysis:

- **Bounce Rate**: The percentage of visitors who leave after viewing one page.
- **Average Session Duration**: Measures how long visitors stay on your site.
- **Pages Per Session**: Indicates the average number of pages viewed during a visit.
- **New vs. Returning Visitors**: Helps understand audience loyalty and repeat traffic.

Segmenting Traffic for Deeper Insights

Segmenting your audience can provide more precise insights:

- **Geographical Segments**: Understand how location impacts behavior.
- **Device Segments**: Compare behaviors across desktops, tablets, and mobile devices.
- **Referral Sources**: Analyze user behavior based on where they came from, such as social media, search engines, or email campaigns.

Creating Data-Driven Strategies

Once the data is collected and analyzed, use the insights to implement changes:

1. **Optimize High-Traffic Pages**: Focus on improving content and design for pages with high traffic but low engagement.
2. **Enhance Conversion Paths**: Simplify navigation and calls-to-action to boost conversions.
3. **Target Underperforming Traffic Sources**: If a source brings in traffic but yields low engagement, reassess the strategy.

Case Studies: Applying User Behavior Insights

Real-world examples can illustrate how user behavior analysis leads to improvements:

- **Example 1**: A blog identified that most readers left after viewing one post. By adding recommended reading sections, session duration increased.
- **Example 2**: An e-commerce site noticed high cart abandonment rates. Optimizing the checkout process reduced drop-offs.

Best Practices for Ongoing Analysis

Analyzing user behavior and traffic is not a one-time task. Regularly reviewing data ensures continued optimization.

- **Set Benchmarks and Goals**: Define clear performance indicators.
- **Regularly Review Metrics**: Schedule weekly or monthly reviews to track progress.

- **Stay Adaptable**: Be ready to adjust strategies based on changing user behaviors or market trends.

CHAPTER 10: LAUNCHING AND MAINTAINING YOUR WEBSITE

Conducting Thorough Pre-Launch Checks

Launching a website is a significant milestone, but the work begins long before the "publish" button is pressed. A meticulous pre-launch process ensures that your site is fully functional, visually appealing, and ready to meet user expectations. Here's a step-by-step guide to help you conduct thorough pre-launch checks.

Understanding the Purpose and Goals of Your Website

Before finalizing any pre-launch tasks, revisit the core purpose of your website. Are you creating an online portfolio, a business site, or an e-commerce platform? Clearly defined goals will guide your pre-launch checklist. For instance, an e-commerce site requires rigorous testing of product pages and payment systems, while a blog must prioritize readability and content organization.

Key Pre-Launch Goals:

- Ensure smooth navigation.
- Optimize for conversions (e.g., sales, sign-ups).
- Deliver an engaging user experience (UX).

Technical Performance Review

A high-performing website is crucial for retaining visitors. Use these steps to ensure your site performs optimally:

1. Page Load Speed:
Page speed significantly impacts user experience and search engine rankings. Use tools like Google PageSpeed Insights or GTmetrix to test loading times and identify bottlenecks.

2. Mobile Responsiveness:
With a majority of users accessing websites via mobile devices, ensure your site adapts seamlessly across various screen sizes. Preview your site on different devices or use online emulators.

3. Cross-Browser Compatibility:
Your site should function consistently on all major browsers, including Chrome, Firefox, Safari, and Edge. Test on multiple versions to catch inconsistencies.

Content Accuracy and Relevance

Quality content is the backbone of any website. Before launching, review every piece of text, image, and video for accuracy and relevance.

1. Proofreading and Editing:
Ensure all content is free of spelling and grammatical errors. Tools like Grammarly or Hemingway can help with this process.

2. Image Optimization:
Compress images without sacrificing quality to ensure fast loading. Use descriptive alt texts for accessibility and SEO benefits.

3. Internal and External Links:

Check that all hyperlinks are functional and direct users to the correct pages. Broken links can frustrate users and harm your site's credibility.

SEO Optimization

Search engine optimization (SEO) enhances your website's visibility. Implement the following tactics before launch:

1. Meta Tags and Descriptions:
Ensure every page has a unique meta title and description that incorporate target keywords.

2. URL Structure:
Use clean, descriptive URLs that reflect the content of each page.

3. XML Sitemap:
Generate an XML sitemap and submit it to search engines to ensure all pages are indexed.

Functionality Testing

Every interactive element on your website should be tested thoroughly:

1. Forms and Submissions:
Test all contact forms, sign-up fields, and feedback mechanisms to ensure data submission works correctly.

2. E-commerce Features (if applicable):
Simulate purchases to verify that the shopping cart, checkout process, and payment gateways function smoothly.

3. Search Functionality:
If your site includes a search bar, ensure it returns accurate and relevant results.

Security Measures

Protecting your site and its users is non-negotiable. Implement robust security measures, such as:

1. SSL Certificate:
Ensure your website has an SSL certificate installed. This not only secures data but also boosts SEO rankings.

2. Password Protection:
Enforce strong passwords for all administrative accounts and encourage users to do the same.

3. Regular Backups:
Set up automated backups to protect your site's data in case of emergencies.

User Experience (UX) and Visual Design Check

An intuitive and visually appealing design keeps visitors engaged. During pre-launch, focus on:

1. Navigation:
Test your menu structure for ease of use. Users should find key pages within three clicks.

2. Design Consistency:
Ensure consistent fonts, colors, and design elements across all pages.

3. Accessibility:
Optimize your site for users with disabilities. This includes adding keyboard navigation, screen reader compatibility, and adequate color contrast.

PUBLISHING THE WEBSITE AND ANNOUNCING THE LAUNCH

Launching a website marks a significant milestone in bringing your online presence to life. After months of designing, optimizing, and refining, the next crucial step is making your website accessible to the public. This phase requires more than a simple click of a "Publish" button; it involves strategic planning to ensure the website launches seamlessly and reaches its intended audience effectively.

Ensuring a Smooth Publishing Process

Before announcing your website launch, it's essential to ensure that the publishing process runs smoothly. This involves verifying technical aspects and ensuring the website is optimized for user experience.

1. Finalizing Design and Functionality

- Double-check that all website components—images, text, and interactive elements—are displayed correctly.
- Ensure that buttons, links, and forms function as intended. Broken links or unresponsive features can frustrate visitors and damage

credibility.

2. Verifying SEO Settings

- Proper SEO settings are crucial for making your website discoverable. Ensure that meta titles, descriptions, and alt text for images are optimized with relevant keywords.
- Submit your sitemap to search engines like Google for indexing.

3. Testing Website Performance

- Use performance tools to evaluate website speed and responsiveness. Address any issues that could hinder the user experience, such as slow loading times or formatting errors on mobile devices.

Crafting an Effective Launch Announcement

1. Identifying Your Target Audience

- Tailor your announcement to resonate with your core audience. Understand their preferences and highlight how your website addresses their needs or interests.

2. Selecting the Right Platforms

- Choose platforms where your audience is most active. Social media, email newsletters, and community forums are excellent channels to generate buzz around your launch.

3. Creating Engaging Content for Announcements

- The announcement should emphasize the value your website offers. Use compelling headlines and visuals to capture attention. For instance, include a sneak peek of unique features or exclusive content available on your site.

4. Incorporating a Call-to-Action (CTA)

- Encourage immediate engagement by including clear CTAs such as "Explore Now," "Sign Up Today," or "Check Out Our Blog." Ensure the CTA links directly to your website to minimize user friction.

Maximizing Reach Post-Launch

After the initial launch, maintaining momentum is critical. Post-launch strategies ensure sustained interest and engagement with your website.

1. Leveraging Social Media

- Share regular updates, such as new blog posts, products, or special offers. Engage with followers by responding to comments and encouraging them to share your content.

2. Collaborating with Influencers and Partners

- Partnering with influencers or related businesses can amplify your reach. They can promote your website to their audience, adding credibility and attracting new visitors.

3. Utilizing Paid Advertising

- Consider running ads on platforms like Google or Facebook to reach a broader audience. Paid ads can be particularly effective for driving traffic and generating leads.

Monitoring Feedback and Analytics

Feedback and performance metrics are essential for refining your website post-launch.

1. Gathering User Feedback

- Implement feedback forms or surveys to understand visitor experiences. Addressing constructive feedback helps improve your website's user experience.

2. Analyzing Traffic and Engagement Data

- Use analytics tools to monitor website performance. Key metrics like bounce rate, session duration, and traffic sources can provide insights into how visitors interact with your site.

3. Continuous Optimization

- Based on feedback and data, make ongoing improvements to your website. Whether it's tweaking design elements or updating content, continual optimization ensures the website remains relevant and effective.

IMPLEMENTING A CONTENT UPDATE STRATEGY

Why Content Updates Matter

Consistently updating your website's content is critical for maintaining relevance, improving search engine rankings, and engaging your audience. Fresh content signals to search engines that your site is active and valuable, improving your visibility online. Moreover, it keeps your audience interested, encouraging return visits and fostering trust.

Key Benefits of Regular Content Updates

1. **Enhanced SEO Performance**
   Search engines prioritize websites with current and relevant content. Updating your blog posts, product descriptions, or service pages can help target new keywords, improve ranking, and increase organic traffic.

2. **Audience Engagement**
   Regular updates, such as news, articles, or fresh visuals, keep your audience engaged and encourage repeat visits. Dynamic content can boost user interaction and build loyalty.

3. **Competitive Edge**
   Keeping your content updated ensures you

remain competitive in your industry. Stale or outdated information may lead users to competitors offering more current and insightful resources.

Developing a Content Update Plan

Creating an effective update strategy involves careful planning. Below are the steps to ensure your content stays fresh and relevant:

1. **Conduct a Content Audit**
   Begin by reviewing your existing content to identify outdated or underperforming pieces. Assess their relevance, accuracy, and performance metrics (traffic, bounce rates, and engagement levels).

2. **Set Clear Objectives**
   Define the purpose of your updates. Are you aiming to increase traffic, improve engagement, or address user feedback? Clear goals will guide your efforts and provide a benchmark for success.

3. **Create an Editorial Calendar**
   Plan updates systematically using an editorial calendar. Include blog posts, case studies, tutorials, or videos that align with your audience's interests. Scheduling ensures consistency and helps manage workload efficiently.

Types of Content to Update

1. **Blog Posts and Articles**

Update older posts with new data, statistics, or insights. Refreshing headlines and images can also enhance their appeal. Repurpose high-performing content by expanding on related topics.

2. **Product or Service Pages**
   Regularly review and refine descriptions, pricing, and features. Highlight new offerings or updates that address evolving customer needs.

3. **Visual and Multimedia Content**
   Replace outdated images or videos with high-quality, relevant media. Adding infographics or tutorials can further enrich the user experience.

4. **Landing Pages**
   Optimize your landing pages by updating calls to action (CTAs), adjusting keywords, and testing different designs for improved conversion rates.

Best Practices for Content Updates

1. **Incorporate Feedback and Analytics**
   Use analytics tools to identify content that underperforms or has high bounce rates. Pay attention to user feedback and address common concerns or suggestions in your updates.

2. **Maintain Consistency in Tone and Style**
   Ensure updates align with your brand's voice and messaging. Consistency fosters familiarity and trust, crucial for audience retention.

3. **Optimize for Mobile Users**
   Given the rise in mobile traffic, ensure your updated content is mobile-friendly. Responsive

designs and fast-loading pages enhance usability on all devices.

4. **Leverage Internal Linking**
Update internal links to direct users to your latest or most relevant content. This strategy improves site navigation and encourages deeper engagement.

Advanced Strategies for Content Updates

1. **Content Personalization**
Use visitor data to tailor content updates for different audience segments. Personalized experiences increase engagement and conversions.

2. **A/B Testing for Optimization**
Experiment with different versions of updated content to determine which performs better. Test variations of headlines, images, and CTAs to refine your approach.

3. **Evergreen Content Creation**
Focus on creating content with long-term relevance. Periodic updates to evergreen content keep it fresh and maintain its value over time.

Measuring the Success of Content Updates

1. **Track Key Performance Indicators (KPIs)**
Monitor metrics such as page views, time on site, and conversion rates to gauge the effectiveness of your updates.

2. **Compare Before and After Performance**
Use historical data to measure the impact of content updates. Look for improvements in traffic, engagement, and search rankings.

3. **Adjust Based on Insights**
   Continuously refine your strategy based on performance data. Adapting to trends and audience preferences ensures sustained success.

MONITORING AND RESPONDING TO USER FEEDBACK

User feedback is the backbone of any successful website. Whether it comes from direct user comments, surveys, or analytics, understanding what visitors think and feel about your site helps refine their experience. A website that listens to its users is more likely to grow and retain its audience.

Understanding the Different Types of User Feedback

1. Direct Feedback

Direct feedback comes from user-initiated communications like contact forms, emails, or comments. This form of feedback is invaluable because it often highlights specific issues users face or areas they appreciate.

Tips for Handling Direct Feedback:

- Respond promptly to inquiries and comments.
- Keep responses polite and professional, even when feedback is negative.
- Use a centralized system for managing user communications to ensure no message gets overlooked.

2. Indirect Feedback

This type includes behavioral data like how long users stay on a page, where they click, or which pages they frequently exit from. Indirect feedback provides insights into user satisfaction without them explicitly stating their opinions.

Leveraging Indirect Feedback:

- Use analytics tools to monitor bounce rates, session durations, and click paths.
- Identify patterns in user behavior to pinpoint potential problem areas or successful content.

3. Solicited Feedback

Solicited feedback is obtained through surveys, polls, or feedback requests. This method allows you to ask specific questions about user experience.

Best Practices for Solicited Feedback:

- Keep surveys short and focused on specific aspects of your site.
- Offer incentives, such as discounts or exclusive content, to encourage participation.
- Regularly review survey responses to spot trends and recurring suggestions.

Tools and Techniques for Collecting Feedback

1. Feedback Forms and Widgets

Embed feedback forms or widgets on your website to encourage visitors to share their thoughts. Tools like Google Forms or built-in website feedback plugins make this easy.

2. Social Media Listening

Monitor your social media channels for comments,

mentions, and messages related to your website. Social media offers a less formal environment where users are often candid about their experiences.

3. Website Analytics Tools
Platforms like Google Analytics or Hotjar provide data on user behavior, helping you interpret indirect feedback. For instance, heatmaps can show which parts of a page users interact with the most.

4. Review Monitoring
If your website has an e-commerce component or user reviews, consistently monitor this feedback. Reviews often contain detailed opinions on specific products or services.

Responding to User Feedback Effectively

1. Acknowledge and Validate Feedback
Users appreciate when their input is recognized. Whether feedback is positive or negative, a simple acknowledgment goes a long way.

Positive Feedback:

- Thank users for their praise and let them know their input is valued.
- Highlight positive comments publicly to encourage similar feedback.

Negative Feedback:

- Apologize for any inconvenience and commit to addressing their concerns.
- Avoid defensive responses; instead, focus on finding a resolution.

2. Prioritize Feedback Based on Impact

Not all feedback warrants immediate action. Prioritize suggestions that significantly affect user experience or align with your business goals.

3. Implement Changes Transparently

If user feedback leads to significant updates or changes, inform your audience. Transparency builds trust and shows users that their opinions matter.

4. Follow Up

Once you've acted on feedback, follow up with the users who provided it. This reinforces their role in shaping your site's evolution and boosts engagement.

Using Feedback to Drive Continuous Improvement

Feedback is not a one-time affair; it's an ongoing cycle that should influence your website's long-term strategy.

1. Regularly Review and Analyze Feedback

Set aside time to review feedback trends. This helps in identifying recurring issues or popular features over time.

2. Iterate Based on Insights

Feedback-driven iterations can range from minor tweaks, like adjusting button placements, to major changes, like redesigning a checkout process.

3. Involve Your Users

Consider running beta tests or focus groups for significant updates. Involving your audience in the development process helps ensure the changes align with their expectations.

Common Pitfalls to Avoid

1. Ignoring Negative Feedback

While it's tempting to focus only on positive comments, negative feedback often contains the most actionable insights.

2. Overreacting to Outliers
Not all feedback is representative of your entire audience. Avoid making drastic changes based on isolated opinions.

3. Lack of Follow-Through
Collecting feedback without implementing changes or communicating your efforts can lead to user frustration. Ensure your feedback process has a clear loop: collect, analyze, act, and communicate.

CHAPTER 11: TROUBLESHOOTING AND FAQS

Understanding Common Website Issues

Even the most well-designed websites can face occasional technical challenges. Identifying common problems and understanding their root causes is the first step toward effective troubleshooting.

1. Loading Speed Issues

- **Cause**: Large image files, unoptimized code, or excessive third-party plugins.
- **Solution**: Compress images, leverage browser caching, and minimize the use of plugins. Regularly check your website's speed using tools like Google PageSpeed Insights.

2. Broken Links

- **Cause**: Outdated URLs or incorrect link inputs.
- **Solution**: Use link-checking tools to identify broken links and update them promptly.

3. Mobile Responsiveness Problems

- **Cause**: Inconsistent design elements or

unresponsive templates.

- **Solution**: Always test your website on multiple devices. Use the built-in mobile preview mode to ensure optimal performance.

4. SEO Underperformance

- **Cause**: Lack of proper meta descriptions, alt text, or keyword optimization.
- **Solution**: Review your SEO settings, update meta tags, and perform keyword research to improve search engine visibility.

Practical Steps for Troubleshooting

When facing technical issues, a systematic approach can save time and effort.

1. Recreate the Problem

- Attempt to replicate the issue in different browsers or devices to narrow down its scope.

2. Review Recent Changes

- Identify any recent updates or modifications that might have triggered the problem. Undoing these changes often resolves the issue.

3. Utilize Built-In Tools

- Most website builders offer diagnostic tools. Use these to scan for potential errors or conflicts.

4. Check Third-Party Integrations

- External widgets or plugins can sometimes interfere with site functionality. Temporarily disable them to isolate the issue.

FAQs for Quick Reference

Q1: Why is my website not appearing on search engines?

- **A**: Ensure your site is indexed by submitting it to search engines. Verify that your privacy settings do not block search engine crawlers.

Q2: What should I do if my site is hacked?

- **A**: Immediately change all passwords, restore your site from a backup, and review your security settings.

Q3: How can I recover lost content?

- **A**: Use the website builder's version history or backup feature to restore previous versions of your site.

Q4: My site displays differently on various browsers. Why?

- **A**: Different browsers may interpret code in unique ways. Test your site on major browsers and adjust your design accordingly.

Preventative Measures for Minimizing Issues

1. Regular Backups

- Schedule automatic backups to ensure you can recover your website quickly in case of data loss.

2. Routine Updates

- Keep all plugins, themes, and software up to date

to benefit from the latest features and security patches.

3. Monitor Site Performance

- Use analytics tools to monitor site traffic and performance metrics, helping you spot potential issues early.

4. Engage with Support Communities

- Join forums or communities related to your website builder. These platforms often have solutions to common problems shared by other users.

WIX SUPPORT AND COMMUNITY RESOURCES

Wix provides a range of support options designed to help users at various stages of website creation and management. These include direct support channels such as email, live chat, and phone support (available depending on your subscription plan). For immediate help, Wix also offers a comprehensive help center featuring articles, tutorials, and step-by-step guides.

Using the Wix Help Center

The **Wix Help Center** serves as the primary resource for troubleshooting common issues. It offers categorized content, covering topics like website setup, customization, SEO, and e-commerce. The search functionality is robust, allowing users to quickly locate answers to specific questions. For example, users struggling with slow load times can search for performance optimization tips.

Leveraging the Wix Community Forum

The **Wix Community Forum** is another valuable resource. It's a platform where users, experts, and Wix staff interact to share experiences and solutions. Common topics include design customization, integration challenges, and troubleshooting technical glitches. This community-driven space often provides insights that aren't covered in the official documentation.

Reaching Out to Customer Support

When self-help resources don't resolve your issue, contacting **Wix Customer Support** is the next step. Premium users often have access to prioritized support options, which can expedite the resolution process. Before reaching out, ensure you have all relevant details at hand, such as the steps leading to the issue, error messages, and screenshots, to help the support team understand and address your problem efficiently.

Top Issues and Solutions

Understanding the most common issues users face and their solutions can save time and frustration. Below are some frequently encountered problems and their fixes:

1. Website Not Displaying Correctly on Mobile
Solution: Use Wix's built-in mobile editor to optimize your site for mobile devices. Ensure all design elements are properly aligned and that text sizes are adjusted for readability.

2. Slow Loading Times
Solution: Compress images, minimize the use of heavy animations, and enable Wix's performance-enhancing tools like lazy loading. Additionally, review and update apps and widgets to ensure they're optimized.

3. Issues with Domain Connection
Solution: Double-check that your domain's DNS settings are correctly configured. Wix provides a detailed guide on connecting domains, and customer support can assist if issues persist.

4. Problems with Payment Integration
Solution: Ensure your payment gateway is correctly set up and supported in your region. Wix offers step-by-step

guidance for configuring popular gateways like PayPal and Stripe.

5. Missing Content After Publishing
Solution: Verify that all changes have been saved and published. If the problem persists, clear your browser cache or try accessing your site from a different device to rule out local caching issues.

Maximizing the Benefits of the Wix Community

Joining Groups and Webinars
Wix frequently hosts webinars and online workshops, which offer real-time learning opportunities. These sessions are ideal for gaining deeper insights into specific features and learning best practices from experts.

Participating in Feature Requests
The Wix community forum also includes a section for feature requests. If you encounter limitations or have ideas for new functionalities, you can submit requests. This is a proactive way to contribute to the platform's development while potentially solving your own challenges.

Tips for Effective Troubleshooting

1. **Document the Issue**: Keep a record of the error, including steps to reproduce it, any error messages, and screenshots.

2. **Search Before Asking**: Many common problems already have solutions available in the Help Center or Community Forum.

3. **Test Across Devices**: Sometimes issues are device-specific. Testing on multiple devices can help isolate the problem.

4. **Stay Updated**: Regularly check for updates to the Wix platform and its features, as updates often resolve known issues.

STAYING UPDATED WITH WIX FEATURES

The digital landscape evolves rapidly, and website platforms like Wix continually update their features to stay competitive. Staying informed about these updates is crucial for maintaining a functional and modern website. This section delves into the methods and resources available to keep users up-to-date with the latest Wix features.

Why Staying Updated is Essential

Wix frequently releases new tools, features, and templates designed to improve website functionality and user experience. Ignoring these updates can result in missed opportunities to enhance your website's performance, aesthetics, or security.

1. **Improved Performance and Efficiency**: Updated features often include performance optimizations that can reduce loading times or enhance compatibility across devices.

2. **Enhanced Security**: Regular updates address security vulnerabilities, protecting your site from potential threats.

3. **New Design Capabilities**: Feature updates may introduce advanced design options, enabling more creative and engaging site layouts.

4. **User Expectations**: Visitors expect modern,

responsive websites. Staying updated ensures your site meets or exceeds these expectations.

Ways to Stay Informed

1. **Wix Blog**

    The Wix blog is an excellent resource for learning about new features and updates. Articles cover a wide range of topics, from new design tools to e-commerce functionalities.

    - **How to Access**: Visit the official Wix website and navigate to the blog section.
    - **Content Highlights**: Updates often come with tutorials or examples demonstrating how to leverage new features effectively.

2. **Release Notes**

    Wix publishes detailed release notes whenever new updates are rolled out. These notes provide a technical overview of what's changed and how it affects existing functionality.

    - **Where to Find**: Available in the Wix Support Center under the "Release Notes" category.
    - **Usage**: Ideal for users seeking a comprehensive understanding of system updates.

3. **Community Forums**

    Wix's community forums are a hub for users to share experiences, ask questions, and discuss updates. Active participation can provide early insights into new features and practical advice from other users.

4. **Webinars and Tutorials**
   Wix frequently hosts webinars and creates video tutorials to guide users through new tools and functionalities. These resources offer visual and interactive learning opportunities.
   - **Access**: Check the "Learn" section on the Wix platform or subscribe to their YouTube channel.
   - **Advantages**: Interactive sessions often allow for real-time questions and demonstrations.

5. **Social Media Channels**
   Following Wix on social media platforms like Twitter, LinkedIn, and Instagram ensures you receive timely announcements about updates and new features.

Best Practices for Adopting New Features

1. **Testing Before Implementation**
   Before integrating a new feature into your live site, test it in a controlled environment. Wix provides tools like preview mode to experiment with updates without affecting your published site.

2. **Evaluate Relevance**
   Not every new feature will suit your website's goals. Carefully evaluate the potential benefits and relevance of each update to ensure it aligns with your needs.

3. **Educate Your Team**
   If multiple people manage your website, ensure everyone is aware of new features

and understands how to use them. Consider organizing brief training sessions or sharing tutorials.

4. **Regularly Review Your Website**
Periodic reviews help identify areas that could benefit from newly introduced features. This proactive approach ensures your site remains modern and efficient.

Troubleshooting Common Update Issues

1. **Compatibility Problems**
Occasionally, new features may not function as expected due to compatibility issues with older site elements or third-party integrations.
   - **Solution**: Consult the Wix Support Center or forums for guidance. In some cases, reverting to a previous version may resolve the issue temporarily.

2. **Learning Curve**
Complex features may require time to learn and implement correctly.
   - **Solution**: Take advantage of Wix's tutorials and community support. Break the learning process into manageable steps.

3. **Bug Reports**
Updates sometimes introduce unforeseen bugs.
   - **Solution**: Report bugs to Wix's support team and monitor release notes for patches or fixes.

CONCLUSION

Recap of Key Takeaways

The journey of building and maintaining a website is filled with opportunities for learning and growth. In this book, we explored essential aspects of creating a professional online presence, starting from foundational steps such as setting up your website interface to more advanced features like optimizing for performance and integrating e-commerce functionalities.

Key insights included:

- **Understanding website basics**: The importance of intuitive design and ease of navigation.
- **Leveraging advanced tools**: Incorporating social media, analytics, and SEO strategies.
- **Enhancing user experience**: Ensuring mobile responsiveness and improving page load speeds.

These takeaways serve as the cornerstone for building a robust website that aligns with your goals, whether personal or professional.

Encouragement to Continue Learning and Improving

Building a website is only the first step; maintaining and evolving it over time is equally crucial. The digital world is dynamic, with trends, tools, and user expectations constantly shifting. Embrace this as a continuous learning journey. Explore new features, test innovative designs, and adapt to the changing needs of your audience.

Remember, every update and improvement you make reflects your commitment to providing value to your users and staying relevant in a competitive online space.

Next Steps for Expanding Your Online Presence

Now that you've established a solid foundation, consider the following steps to broaden your online impact:

1. **Dive into Advanced Analytics**
   Use data-driven insights to understand user behavior, track performance, and identify areas for improvement. This can help you make informed decisions about content, design, and marketing strategies.

2. **Explore E-commerce Opportunities**
   If applicable, add an online store to your website. Experiment with different product offerings, payment gateways, and promotional strategies to enhance revenue streams.

3. **Engage with Your Audience**
   Strengthen connections by maintaining a blog, hosting webinars, or running email marketing campaigns. Consistent communication builds trust and loyalty.

4. **Stay Updated on Industry Trends**
   Follow industry blogs, participate in forums, and join professional networks to stay informed about the latest developments in website creation and digital marketing.

5. **Invest in Continued Education**
   Consider taking courses or attending workshops

to deepen your skills in web development, design, or online marketing. Mastering these areas will empower you to push your website to new heights.

www.ingramcontent.com/pod-product-compliance
Lightning Source LLC
Chambersburg PA
CBHW071545220526
45469CB00003B/929